Nuclear Winter

VOLUME THREE

BOOM! BOX

ROSS RICHIE..CEO & Founder
JOY HUFFMAN..CFO
MATT GAGNON...Editor-in-Chief
FILIP SABLIK..........................President, Publishing & Marketing
STEPHEN CHRISTY..............................President, Development
LANCE KREITER.........Vice President, Licensing & Merchandising
ARUNE SINGH...Vice President, Marketing
BRYCE CARLSON.....Vice President, Editorial & Creative Strategy
SCOTT NEWMAN...........................Manager, Production Design
KATE HENNING.......................................Manager, Operations
SPENCER SIMPSON..Manager, Sales
SIERRA HAHN..Executive Editor
JEANINE SCHAEFER..Executive Editor
DAFNA PLEBAN...Senior Editor
SHANNON WATTERS...Senior Editor
ERIC HARBURN...Editor
CHRIS ROSA...Editor
MATTHEW LEVINE...Associate Editor
SOPHIE PHILIPS-ROBERTS...............................Assistant Editor
GAVIN GRONENTHAL...Assistant Editor
MICHAEL MOCCIO..Assistant Editor

GWEN WALLER...Assistant Editor
AMANDA LaFRANCO...Executive Assistant
JILLIAN CRAB...Design Coordinator
MICHELLE ANKLEY...Design Coordinator
KARA LEOPARD..Production Designer
MARIE KRUPINA...Production Designer
GRACE PARK..Production Designer
CHELSEA ROBERTS.................................Production Design Assistant
SAMANTHA KNAPP.................................Production Design Assistant
JOSÉ MEZA..Live Events Lead
STEPHANIE HOCUTT..Digital Marketing Lead
ESTHER KIM...Marketing Coordinator
CAT O'GRADY..Digital Marketing Coordinator
AMANDA LAWSON..Marketing Assistant
HOLLY AITCHISON.......................................Digital Sales Coordinator
MORGAN PERRY...Retail Sales Coordinator
MEGAN CHRISTOPHER......................................Operations Coordinator
RODRIGO HERNANDEZ...Mailroom Assistant
ZIPPORAH SMITH..Marketing Assistant
BREANNA SARPY...Executive Assistant

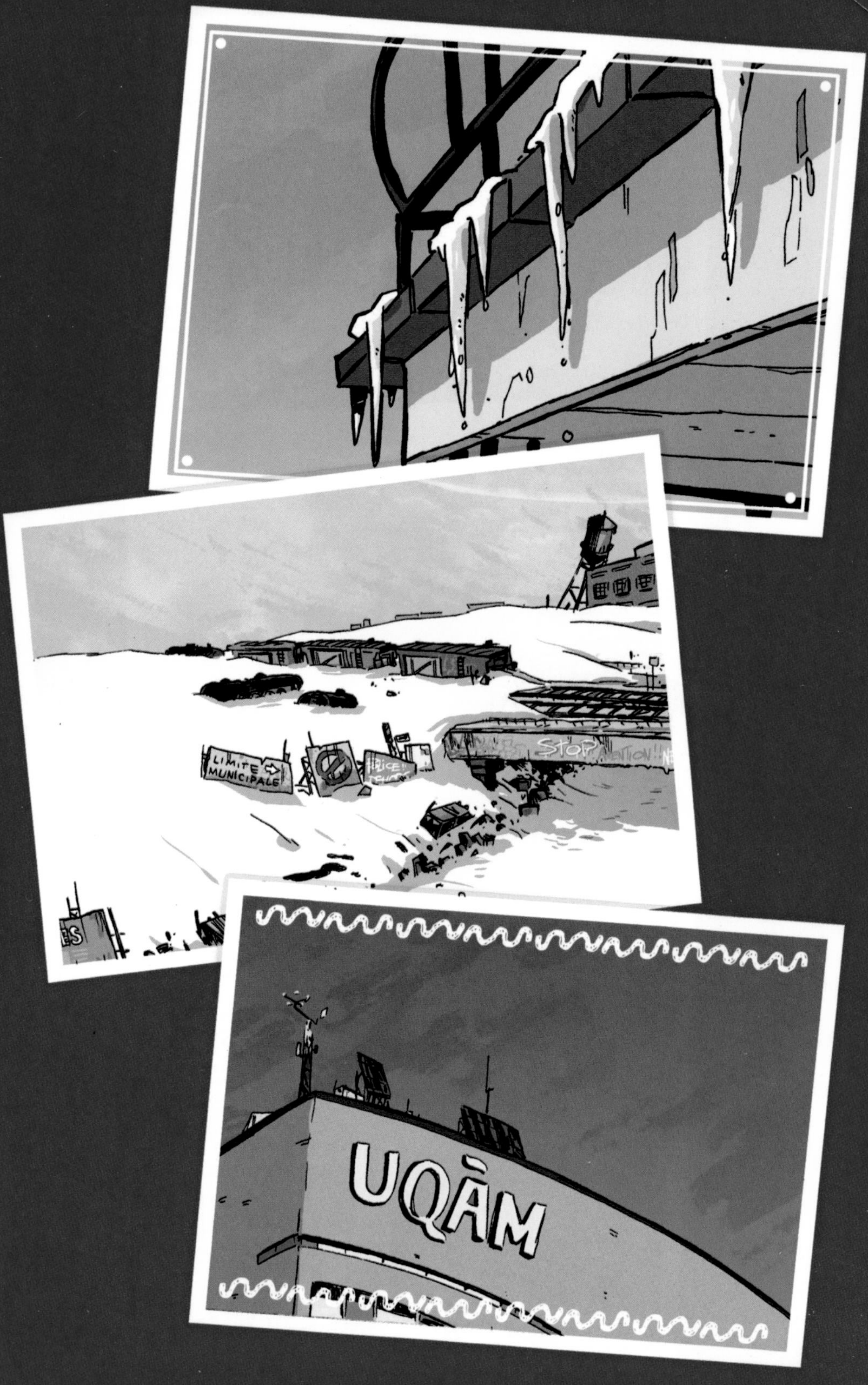
LIMITE MUNICIPALE
STOP
ATTENTION!!
UQÀM

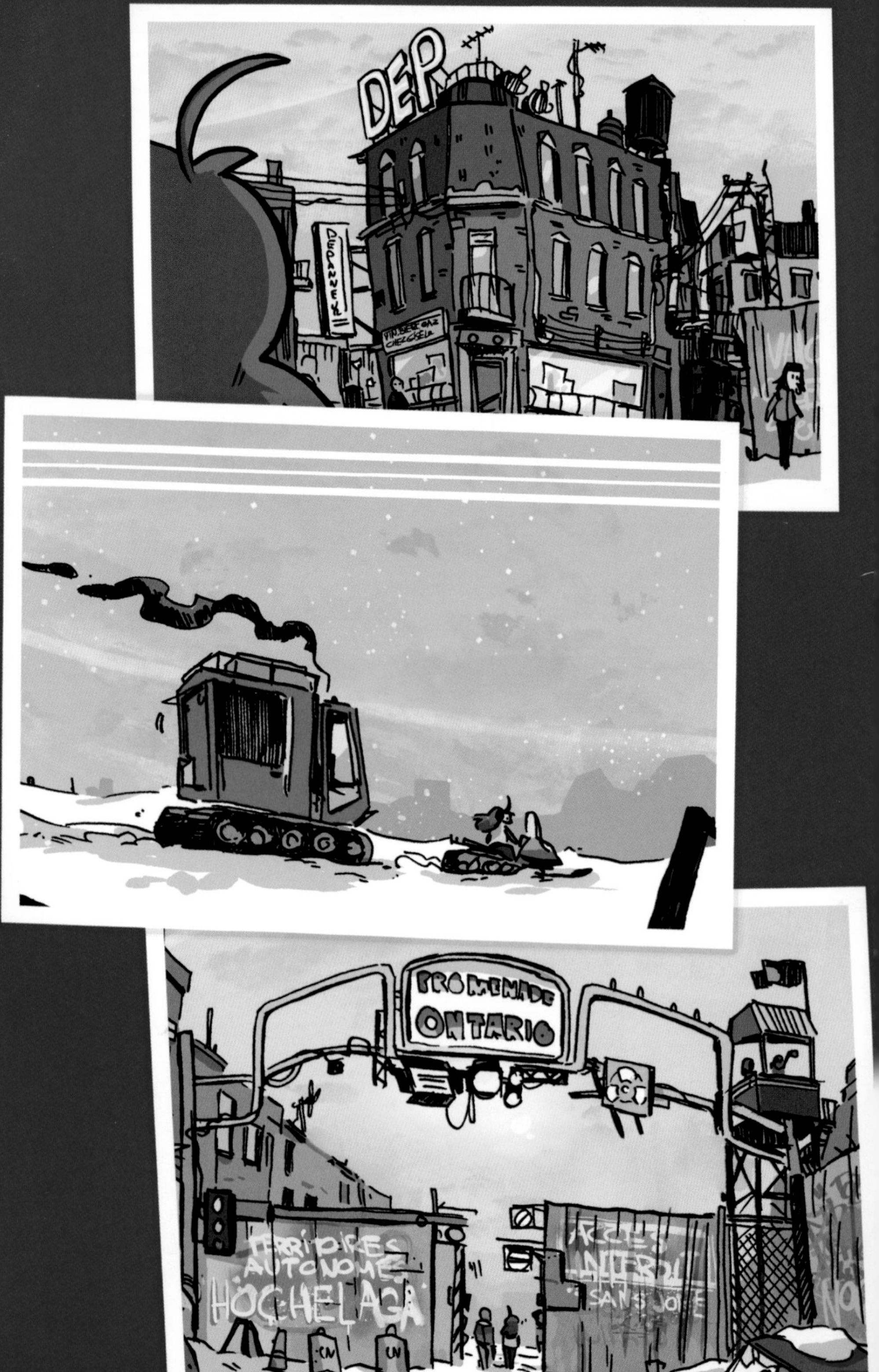
DEP
DEPANNEUR
VIN BIERE GAZ
CHEZ GISELA
PROMENADE
ONTARIO
TERRITOIRES
AUTONOMES
HOÇHELAGA
CN
CN

Written & Illustrated by
Cab

English Translation by
Edward Gauvin

Letters by
Deron Bennett

Designer
Chelsea Roberts

Assistant Editor
Michael Moccio

Editor
Shannon Watters

CHAPTER 1
NIGHT CLASS

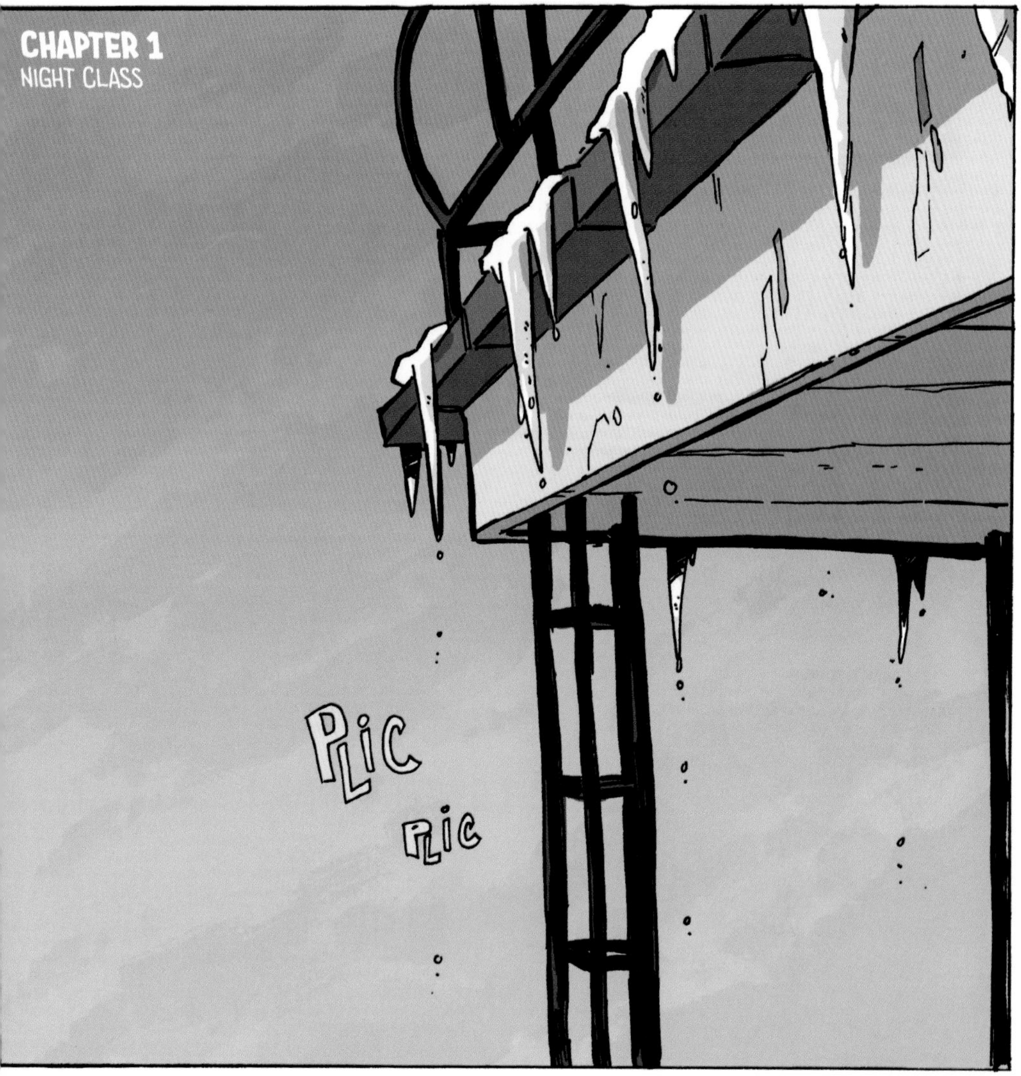
PLIC
PLIC

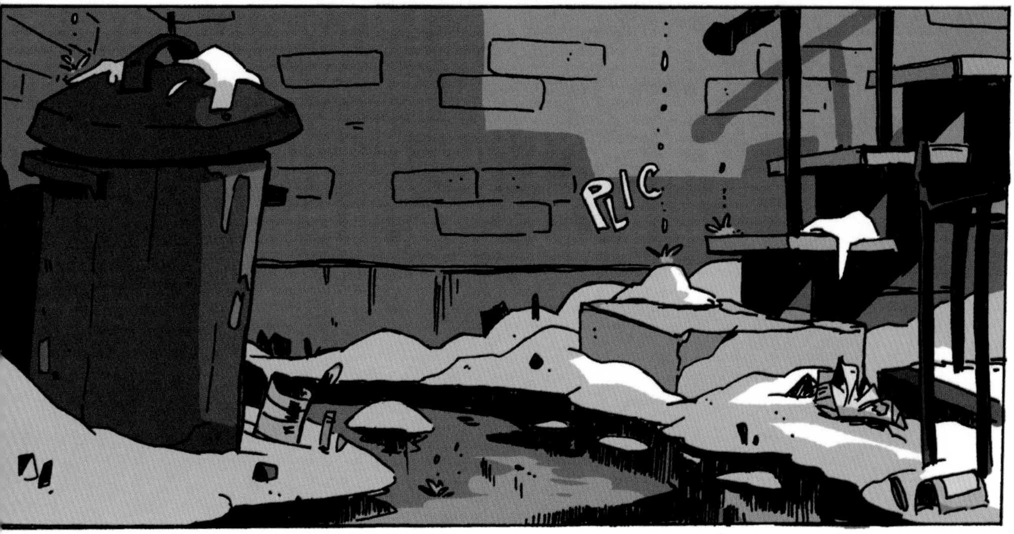
PLIC

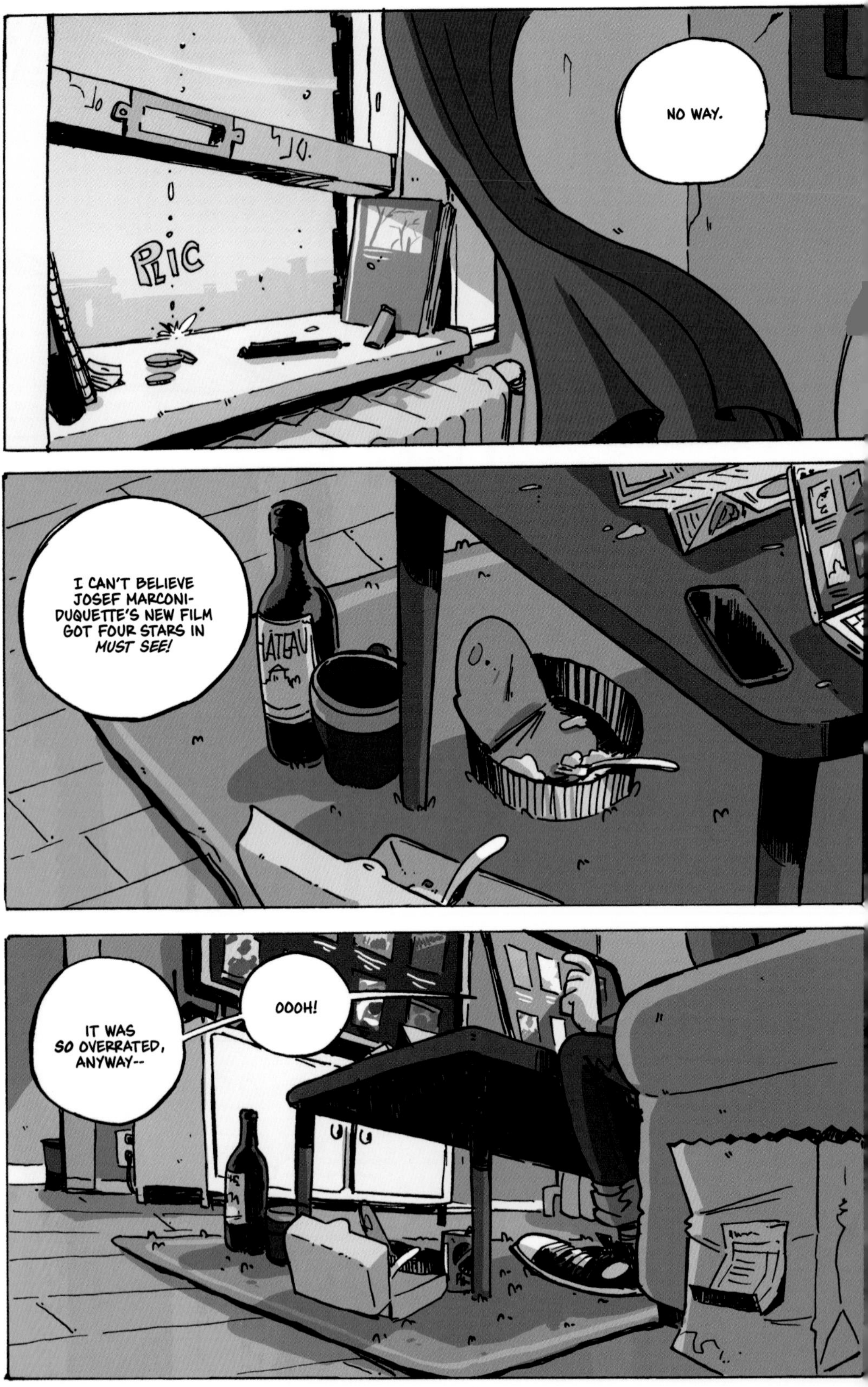
PLIC
NO WAY.
I CAN'T BELIEVE JOSEF MARCONI-DUQUETTE'S NEW FILM GOT FOUR STARS IN *MUST SEE!*
IT WAS SO OVERRATED, ANYWAY--
OOOH!

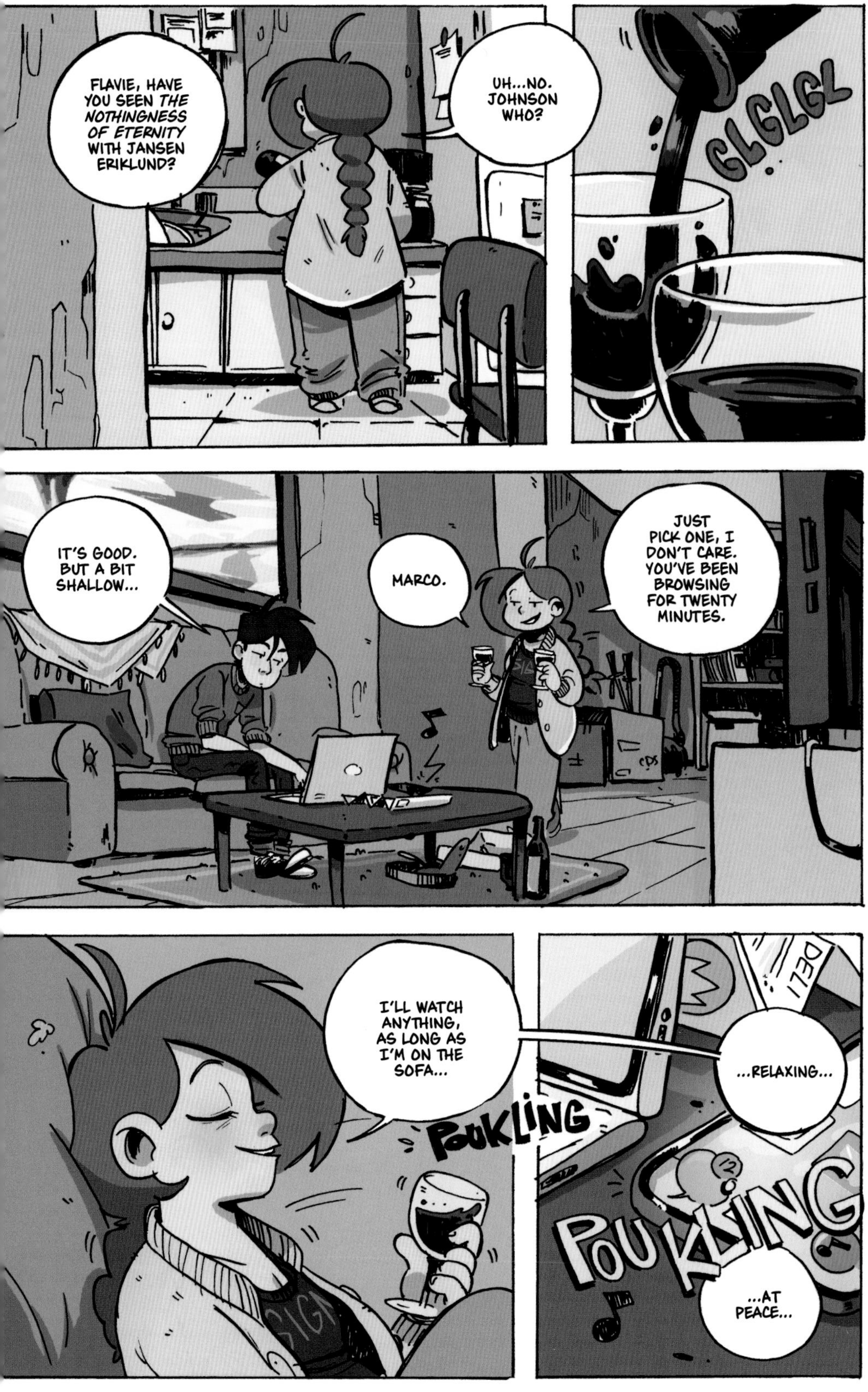
FLAVIE, HAVE YOU SEEN *THE NOTHINGNESS OF ETERNITY* WITH JANSEN ERIKLUND?
UH...NO. JOHNSON WHO?
GLGLGL
IT'S GOOD. BUT A BIT SHALLOW...
MARCO.
JUST PICK ONE, I DON'T CARE. YOU'VE BEEN BROWSING FOR TWENTY MINUTES.
I'LL WATCH ANYTHING, AS LONG AS I'M ON THE SOFA...
...RELAXING...
POUKLING
DELI
POUKLING
...AT PEACE...

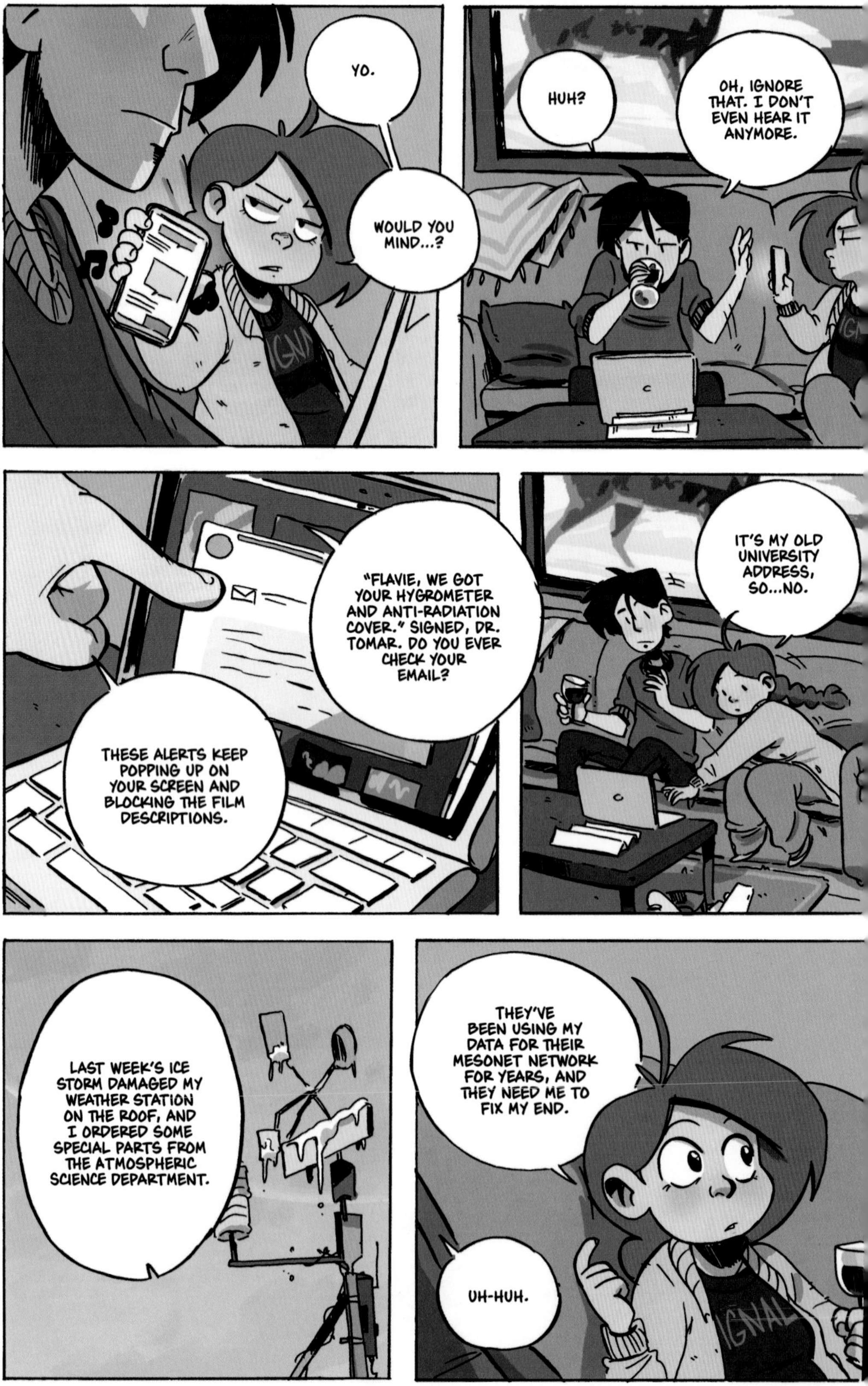
YO.
WOULD YOU MIND...?
HUH?
OH, IGNORE THAT. I DON'T EVEN HEAR IT ANYMORE.
"FLAVIE, WE GOT YOUR HYGROMETER AND ANTI-RADIATION COVER." SIGNED, DR. TOMAR. DO YOU EVER CHECK YOUR EMAIL?
THESE ALERTS KEEP POPPING UP ON YOUR SCREEN AND BLOCKING THE FILM DESCRIPTIONS.
IT'S MY OLD UNIVERSITY ADDRESS, SO...NO.
LAST WEEK'S ICE STORM DAMAGED MY WEATHER STATION ON THE ROOF, AND I ORDERED SOME SPECIAL PARTS FROM THE ATMOSPHERIC SCIENCE DEPARTMENT.
THEY'VE BEEN USING MY DATA FOR THEIR MESONET NETWORK FOR YEARS, AND THEY NEED ME TO FIX MY END.
UH-HUH.

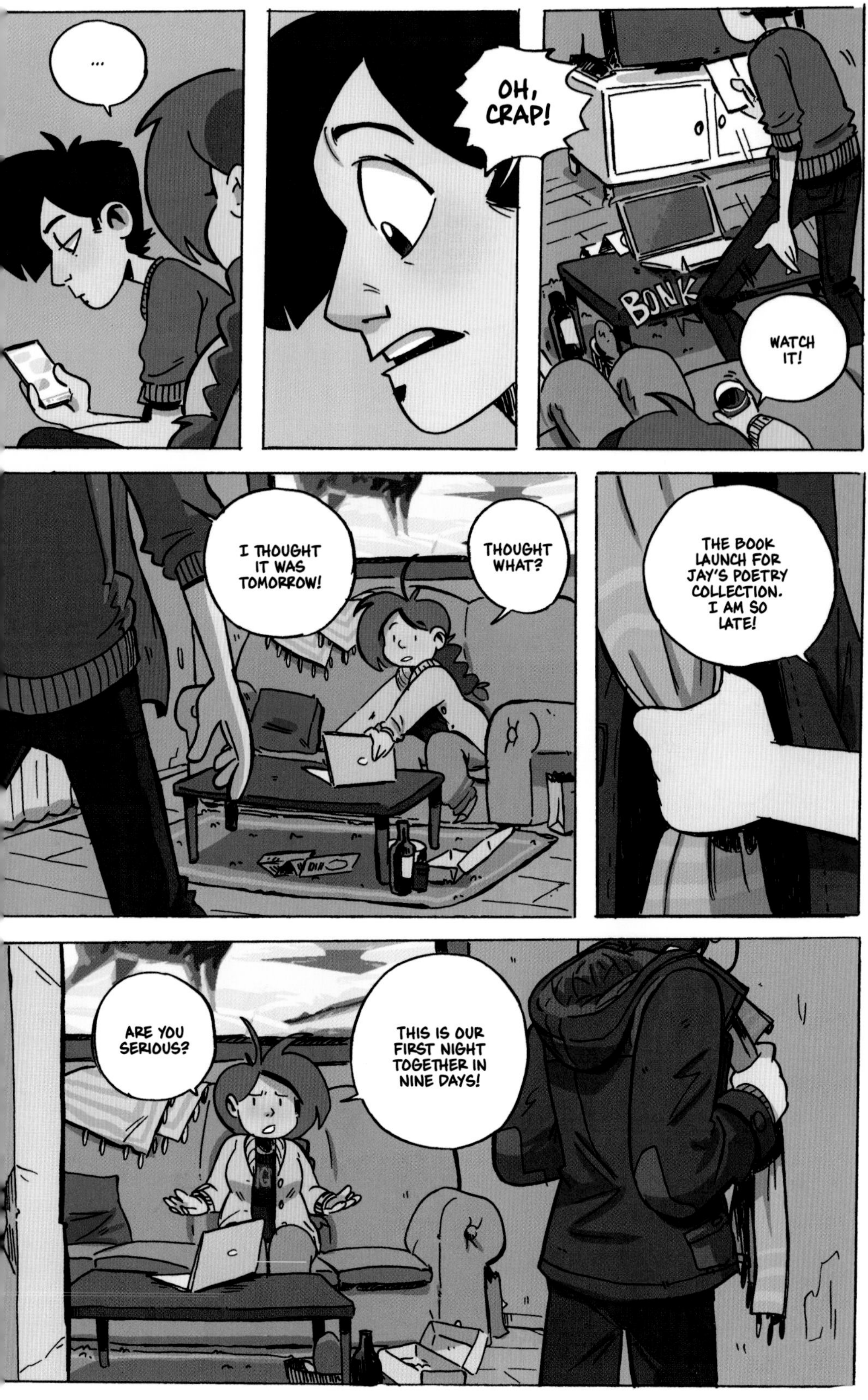
...
OH, CRAP!
BONK
WATCH IT!
I THOUGHT IT WAS TOMORROW!
THOUGHT WHAT?
THE BOOK LAUNCH FOR JAY'S POETRY COLLECTION. I AM SO LATE!
ARE YOU SERIOUS?
THIS IS OUR FIRST NIGHT TOGETHER IN NINE DAYS!

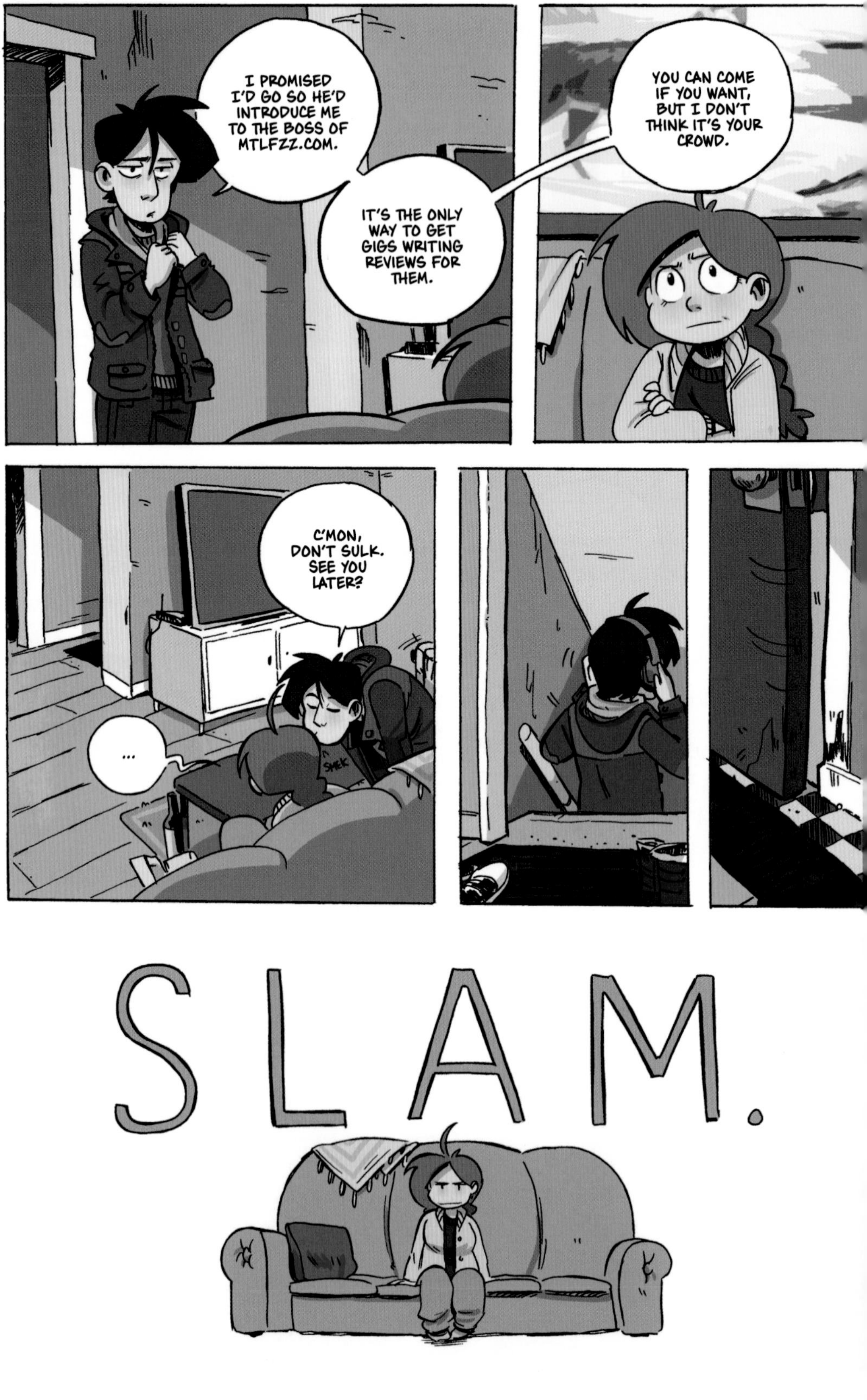
I PROMISED I'D GO SO HE'D INTRODUCE ME TO THE BOSS OF MTLFZZ.COM.
IT'S THE ONLY WAY TO GET GIGS WRITING REVIEWS FOR THEM.
YOU CAN COME IF YOU WANT, BUT I DON'T THINK IT'S YOUR CROWD.
C'MON, DON'T SULK. SEE YOU LATER?
SMEK
...
SLAM.

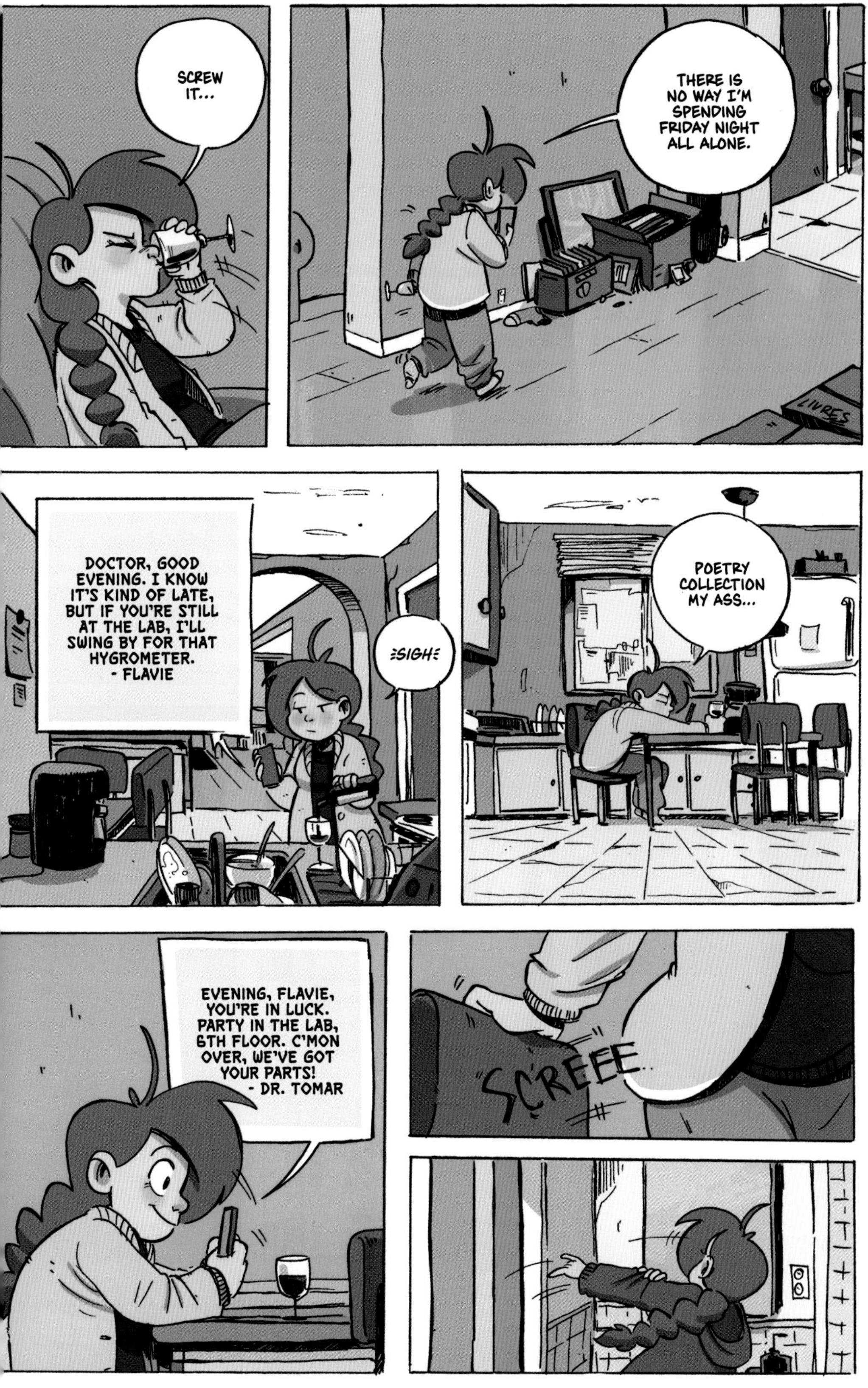
SCREW IT...
THERE IS NO WAY I'M SPENDING FRIDAY NIGHT ALL ALONE.
LIVRES
DOCTOR, GOOD EVENING. I KNOW IT'S KIND OF LATE, BUT IF YOU'RE STILL AT THE LAB, I'LL SWING BY FOR THAT HYGROMETER.
- FLAVIE
SIGH
POETRY COLLECTION MY ASS...
EVENING, FLAVIE, YOU'RE IN LUCK. PARTY IN THE LAB, 6TH FLOOR. C'MON OVER, WE'VE GOT YOUR PARTS!
- DR. TOMAR
SCREEE

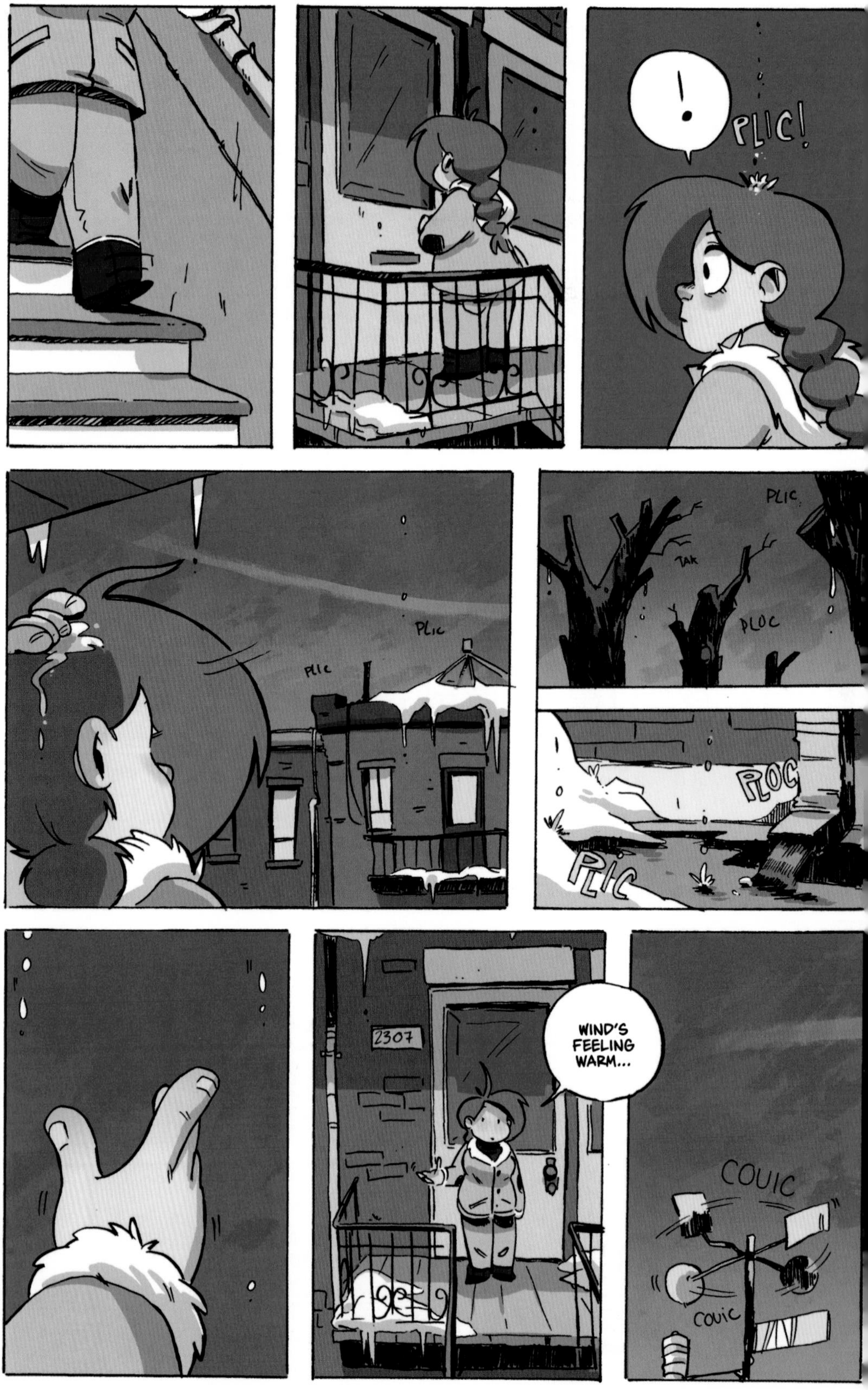

!
PLIC!
PLIC
PLIC
PLIC
TAK
PLOC
PLOC
PLIC
2307
WIND'S FEELING WARM...
COUIC
COUIC

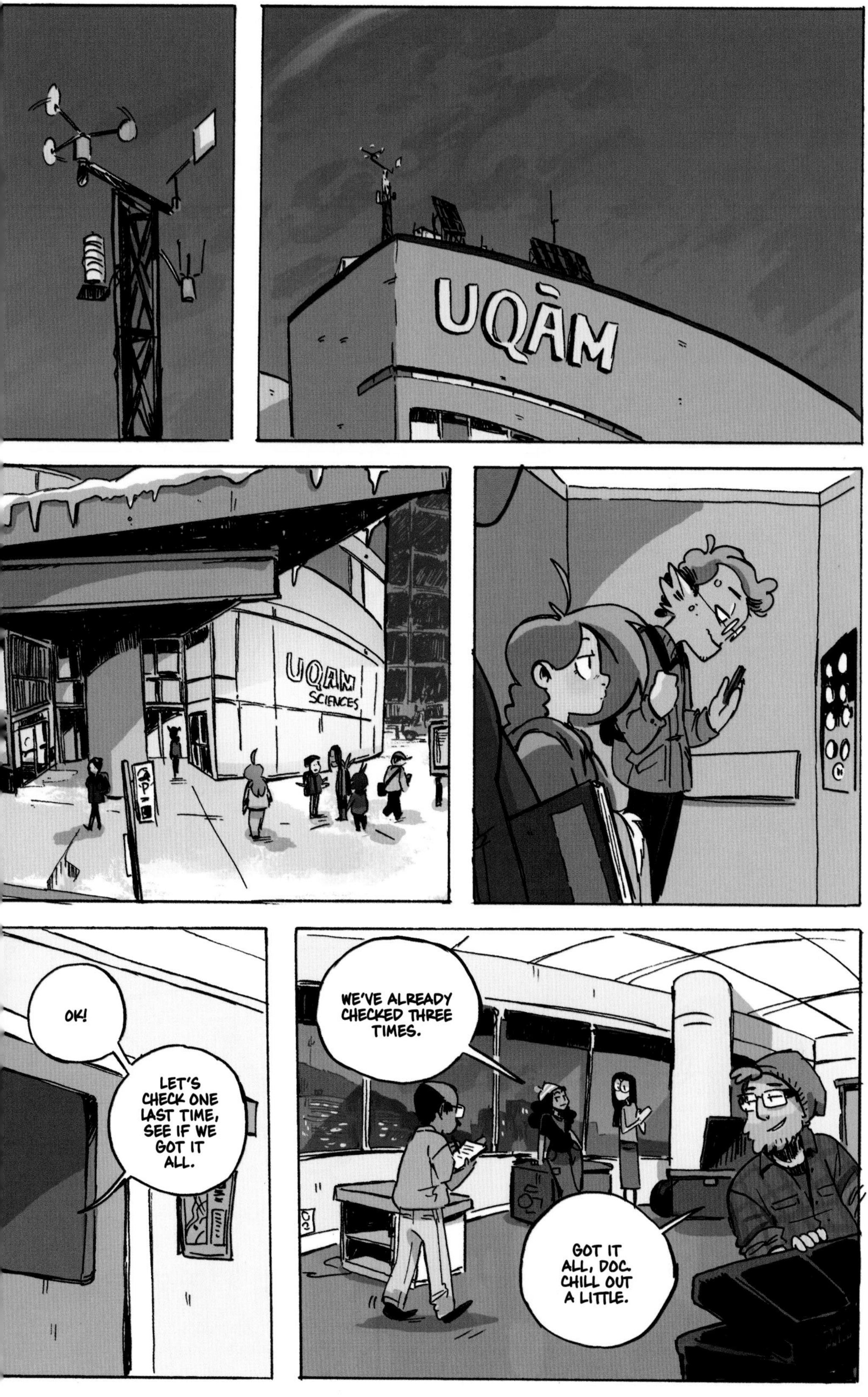
UQÀM
UQAM SCIENCES
OK!
LET'S CHECK ONE LAST TIME, SEE IF WE GOT IT ALL.
WE'VE ALREADY CHECKED THREE TIMES.
GOT IT ALL, DOC. CHILL OUT A LITTLE.

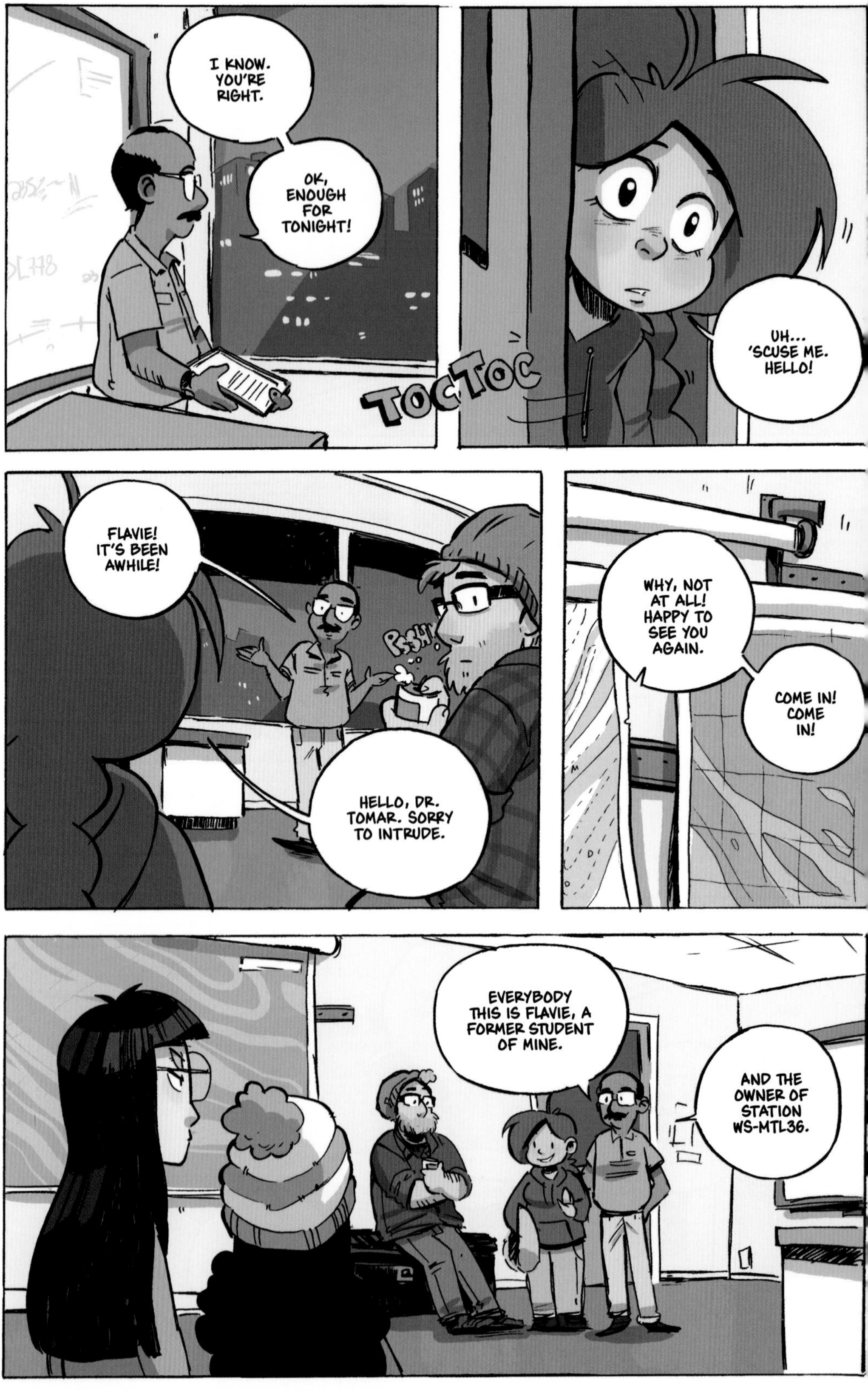
I KNOW. YOU'RE RIGHT.
OK, ENOUGH FOR TONIGHT!
TOCTOC
UH... 'SCUSE ME. HELLO!
FLAVIE! IT'S BEEN AWHILE!
PSSHT!
HELLO, DR. TOMAR. SORRY TO INTRUDE.
WHY, NOT AT ALL! HAPPY TO SEE YOU AGAIN.
COME IN! COME IN!
EVERYBODY THIS IS FLAVIE, A FORMER STUDENT OF MINE.
AND THE OWNER OF STATION WS-MTL36.

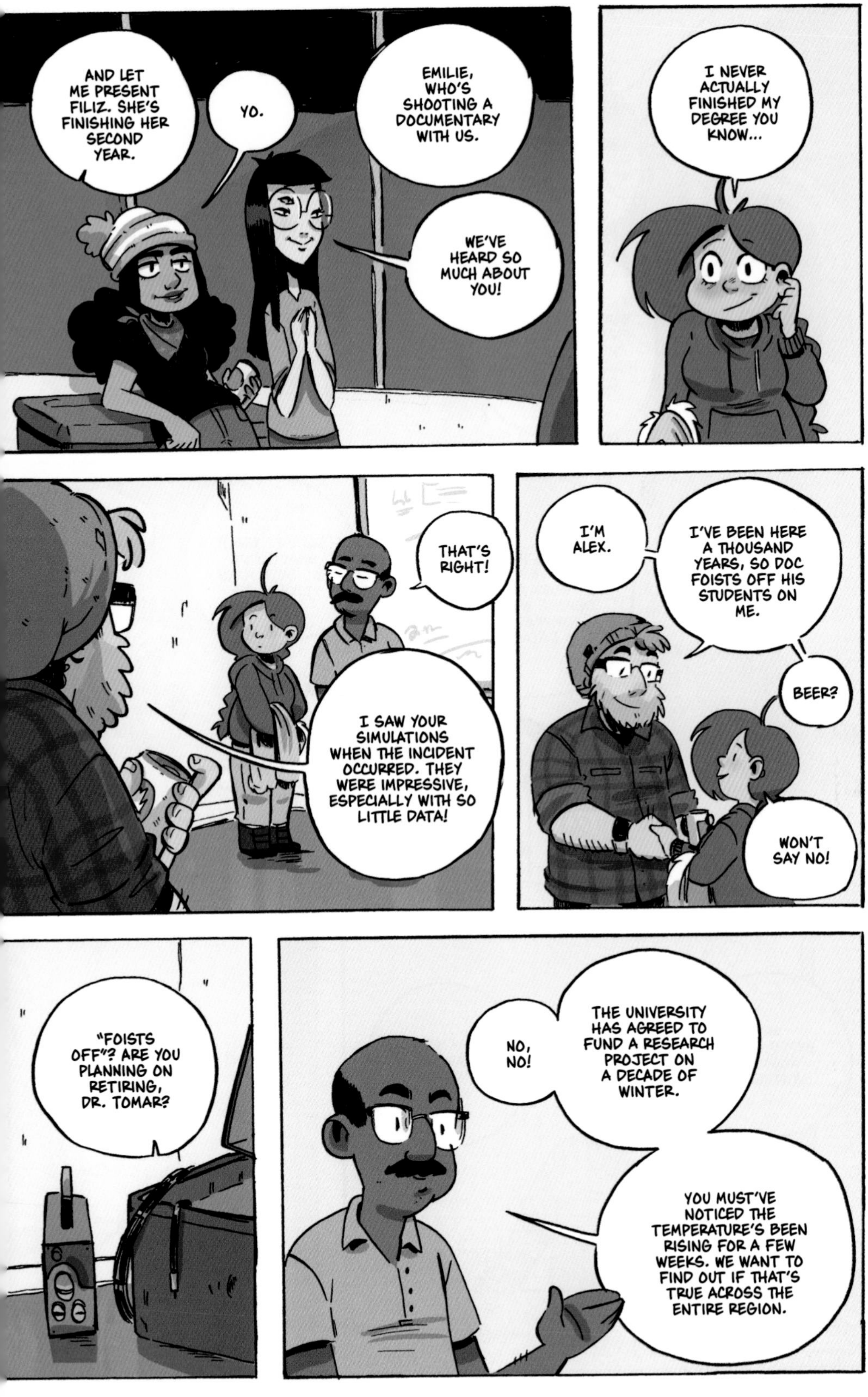
AND LET ME PRESENT FILIZ. SHE'S FINISHING HER SECOND YEAR.
YO.
EMILIE, WHO'S SHOOTING A DOCUMENTARY WITH US.
WE'VE HEARD SO MUCH ABOUT YOU!
I NEVER ACTUALLY FINISHED MY DEGREE YOU KNOW...
THAT'S RIGHT!
I SAW YOUR SIMULATIONS WHEN THE INCIDENT OCCURRED. THEY WERE IMPRESSIVE, ESPECIALLY WITH SO LITTLE DATA!
I'M ALEX.
I'VE BEEN HERE A THOUSAND YEARS, SO DOC FOISTS OFF HIS STUDENTS ON ME.
BEER?
WON'T SAY NO!
"FOISTS OFF"? ARE YOU PLANNING ON RETIRING, DR. TOMAR?
NO, NO!
THE UNIVERSITY HAS AGREED TO FUND A RESEARCH PROJECT ON A DECADE OF WINTER.
YOU MUST'VE NOTICED THE TEMPERATURE'S BEEN RISING FOR A FEW WEEKS. WE WANT TO FIND OUT IF THAT'S TRUE ACROSS THE ENTIRE REGION.

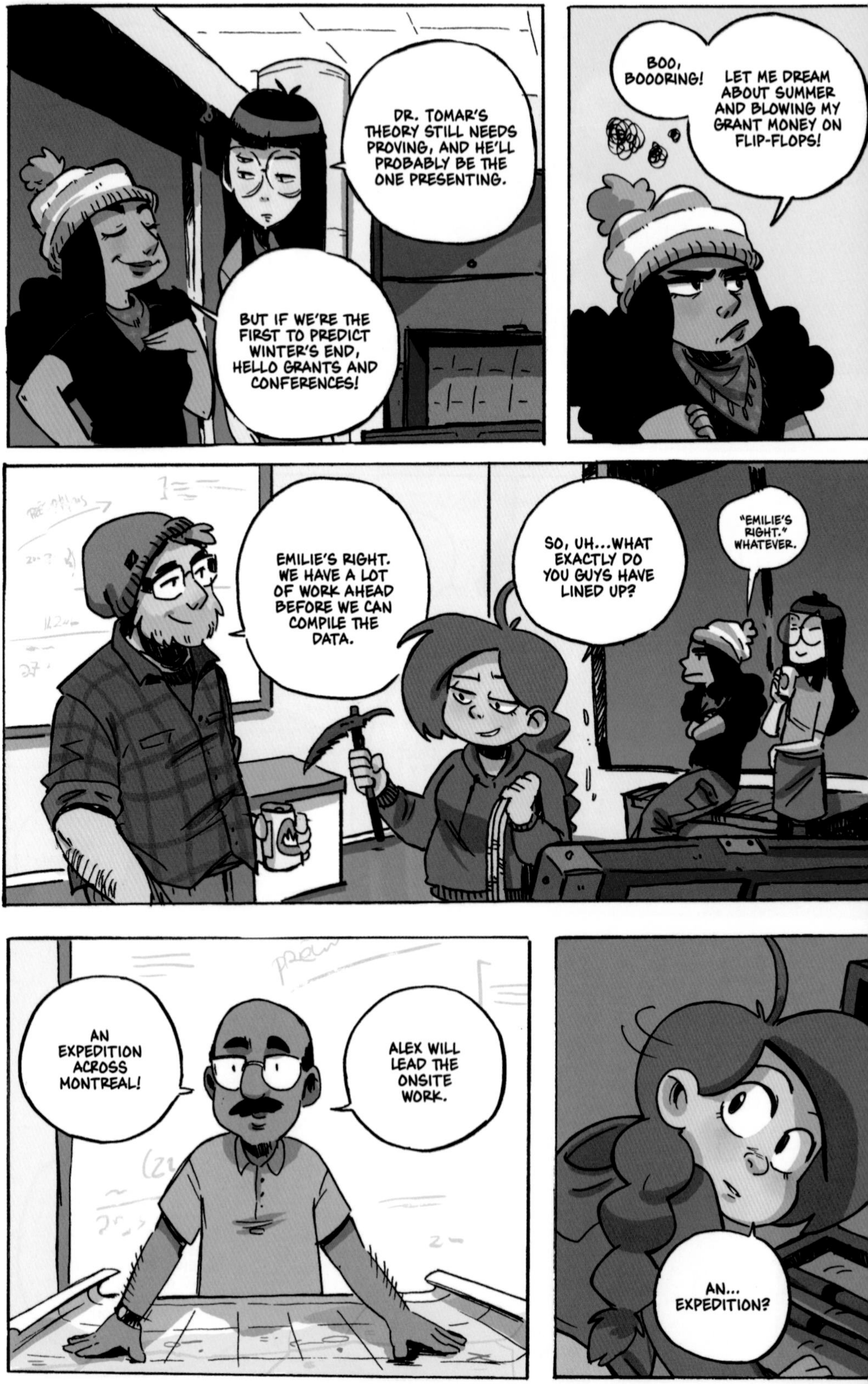
DR. TOMAR'S THEORY STILL NEEDS PROVING, AND HE'LL PROBABLY BE THE ONE PRESENTING.
BUT IF WE'RE THE FIRST TO PREDICT WINTER'S END, HELLO GRANTS AND CONFERENCES!
BOO, BOOORING!
LET ME DREAM ABOUT SUMMER AND BLOWING MY GRANT MONEY ON FLIP-FLOPS!
EMILIE'S RIGHT. WE HAVE A LOT OF WORK AHEAD BEFORE WE CAN COMPILE THE DATA.
SO, UH...WHAT EXACTLY DO YOU GUYS HAVE LINED UP?
"EMILIE'S RIGHT." WHATEVER.
AN EXPEDITION ACROSS MONTREAL!
ALEX WILL LEAD THE ONSITE WORK.
AN... EXPEDITION?

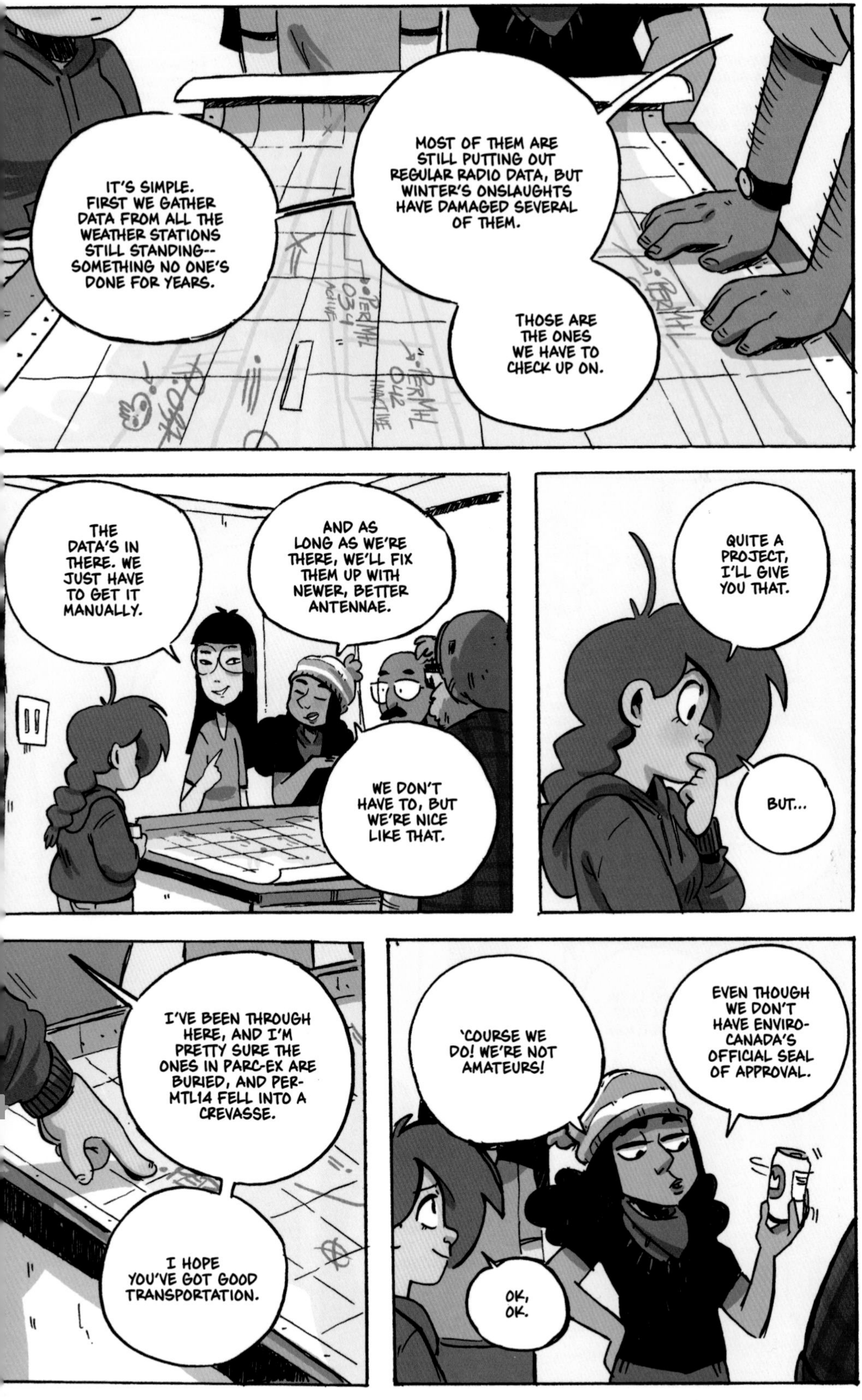
IT'S SIMPLE. FIRST WE GATHER DATA FROM ALL THE WEATHER STATIONS STILL STANDING-- SOMETHING NO ONE'S DONE FOR YEARS.
MOST OF THEM ARE STILL PUTTING OUT REGULAR RADIO DATA, BUT WINTER'S ONSLAUGHTS HAVE DAMAGED SEVERAL OF THEM.
THOSE ARE THE ONES WE HAVE TO CHECK UP ON.
THE DATA'S IN THERE. WE JUST HAVE TO GET IT MANUALLY.
AND AS LONG AS WE'RE THERE, WE'LL FIX THEM UP WITH NEWER, BETTER ANTENNAE.
WE DON'T HAVE TO, BUT WE'RE NICE LIKE THAT.
QUITE A PROJECT, I'LL GIVE YOU THAT.
BUT...
I'VE BEEN THROUGH HERE, AND I'M PRETTY SURE THE ONES IN PARC-EX ARE BURIED, AND PER-MTL14 FELL INTO A CREVASSE.
I HOPE YOU'VE GOT GOOD TRANSPORTATION.
'COURSE WE DO! WE'RE NOT AMATEURS!
EVEN THOUGH WE DON'T HAVE ENVIRO-CANADA'S OFFICIAL SEAL OF APPROVAL.
OK, OK.

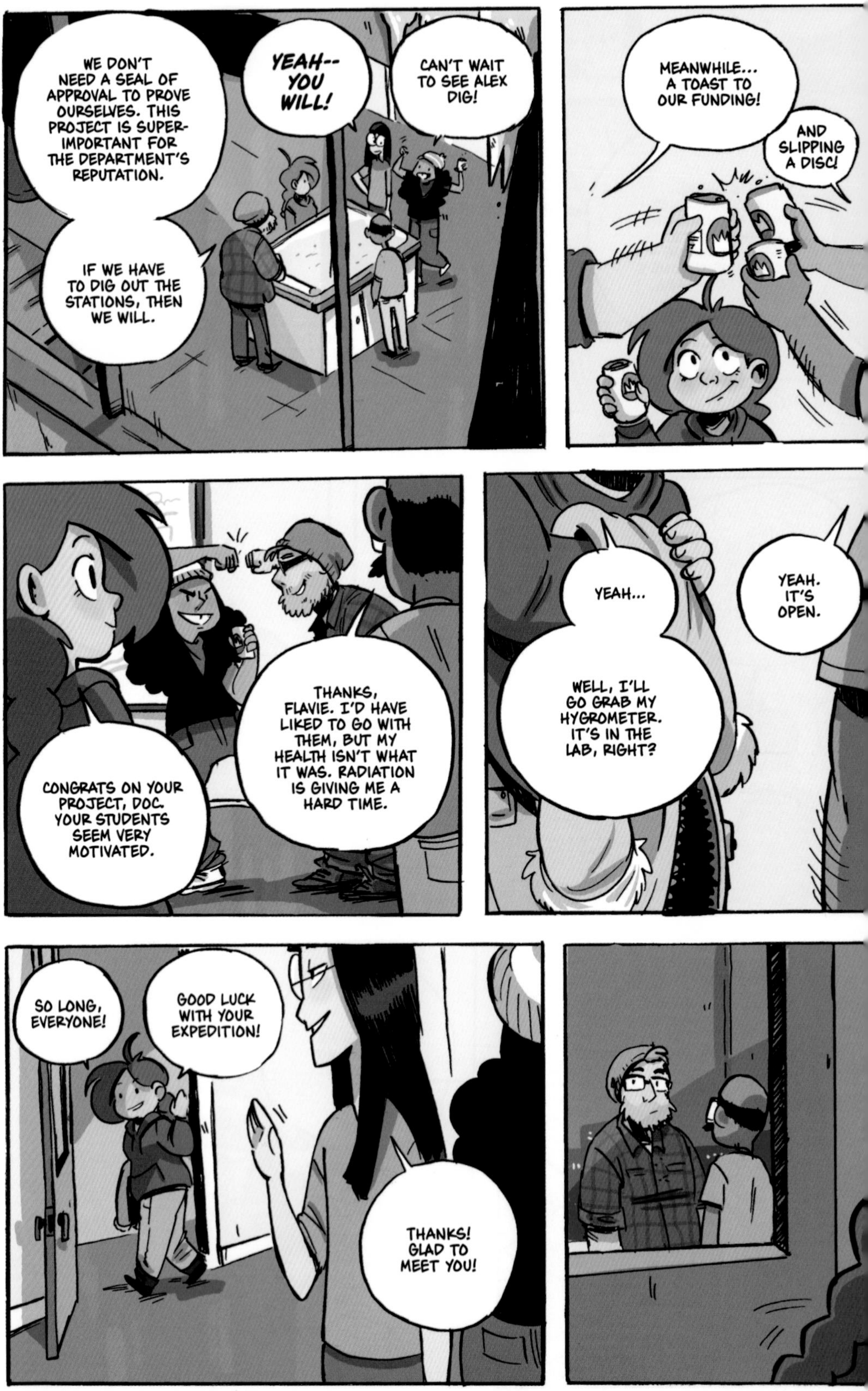
WE DON'T NEED A SEAL OF APPROVAL TO PROVE OURSELVES. THIS PROJECT IS SUPER-IMPORTANT FOR THE DEPARTMENT'S REPUTATION.
IF WE HAVE TO DIG OUT THE STATIONS, THEN WE WILL.
YEAH-- YOU WILL!
CAN'T WAIT TO SEE ALEX DIG!
MEANWHILE... A TOAST TO OUR FUNDING!
AND SLIPPING A DISC!
CONGRATS ON YOUR PROJECT, DOC. YOUR STUDENTS SEEM VERY MOTIVATED.
THANKS, FLAVIE. I'D HAVE LIKED TO GO WITH THEM, BUT MY HEALTH ISN'T WHAT IT WAS. RADIATION IS GIVING ME A HARD TIME.
YEAH...
WELL, I'LL GO GRAB MY HYGROMETER. IT'S IN THE LAB, RIGHT?
YEAH. IT'S OPEN.
SO LONG, EVERYONE!
GOOD LUCK WITH YOUR EXPEDITION!
THANKS! GLAD TO MEET YOU!

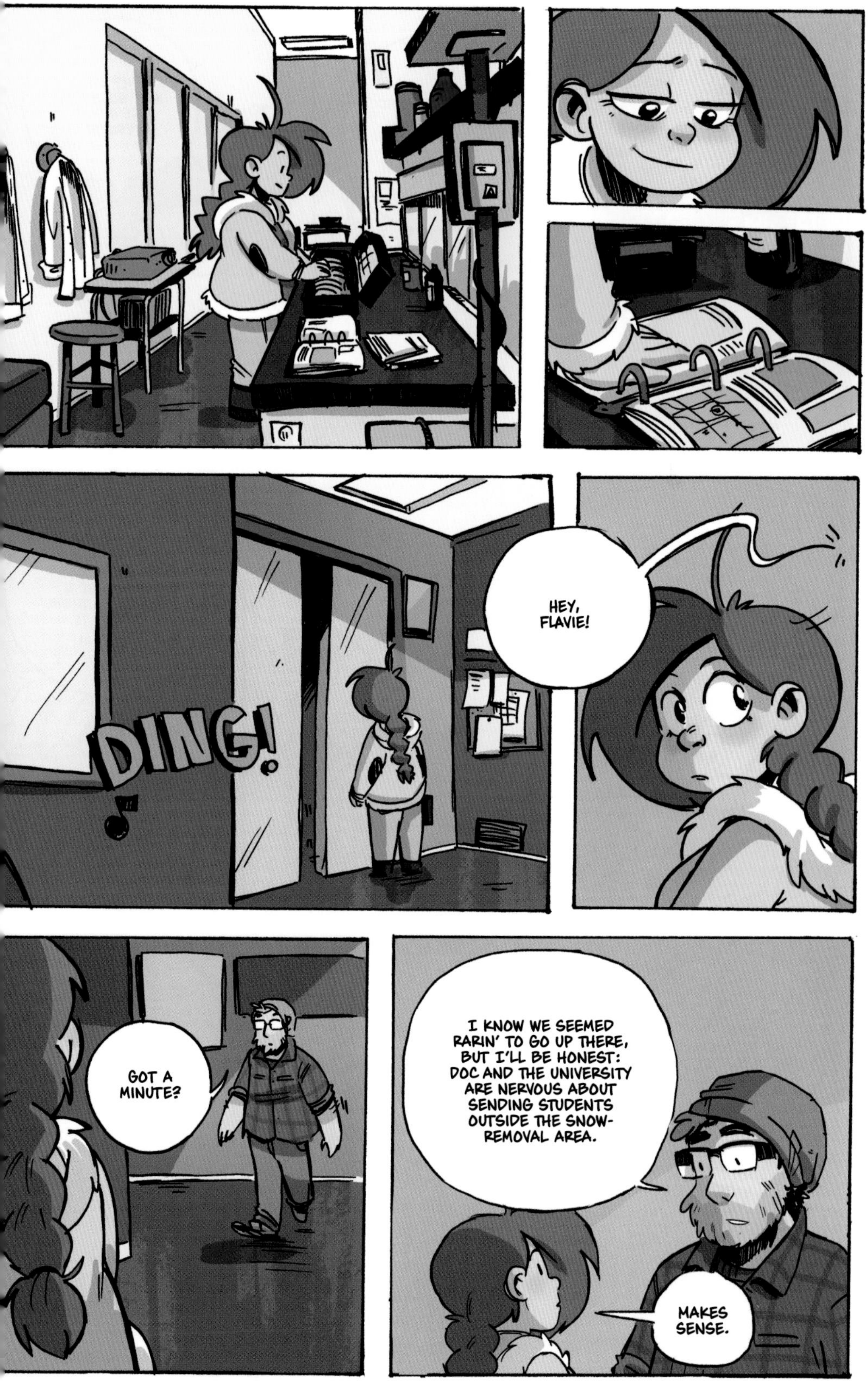
DING!
HEY, FLAVIE!
GOT A MINUTE?
I KNOW WE SEEMED RARIN' TO GO UP THERE, BUT I'LL BE HONEST: DOC AND THE UNIVERSITY ARE NERVOUS ABOUT SENDING STUDENTS OUTSIDE THE SNOW-REMOVAL AREA.
MAKES SENSE.

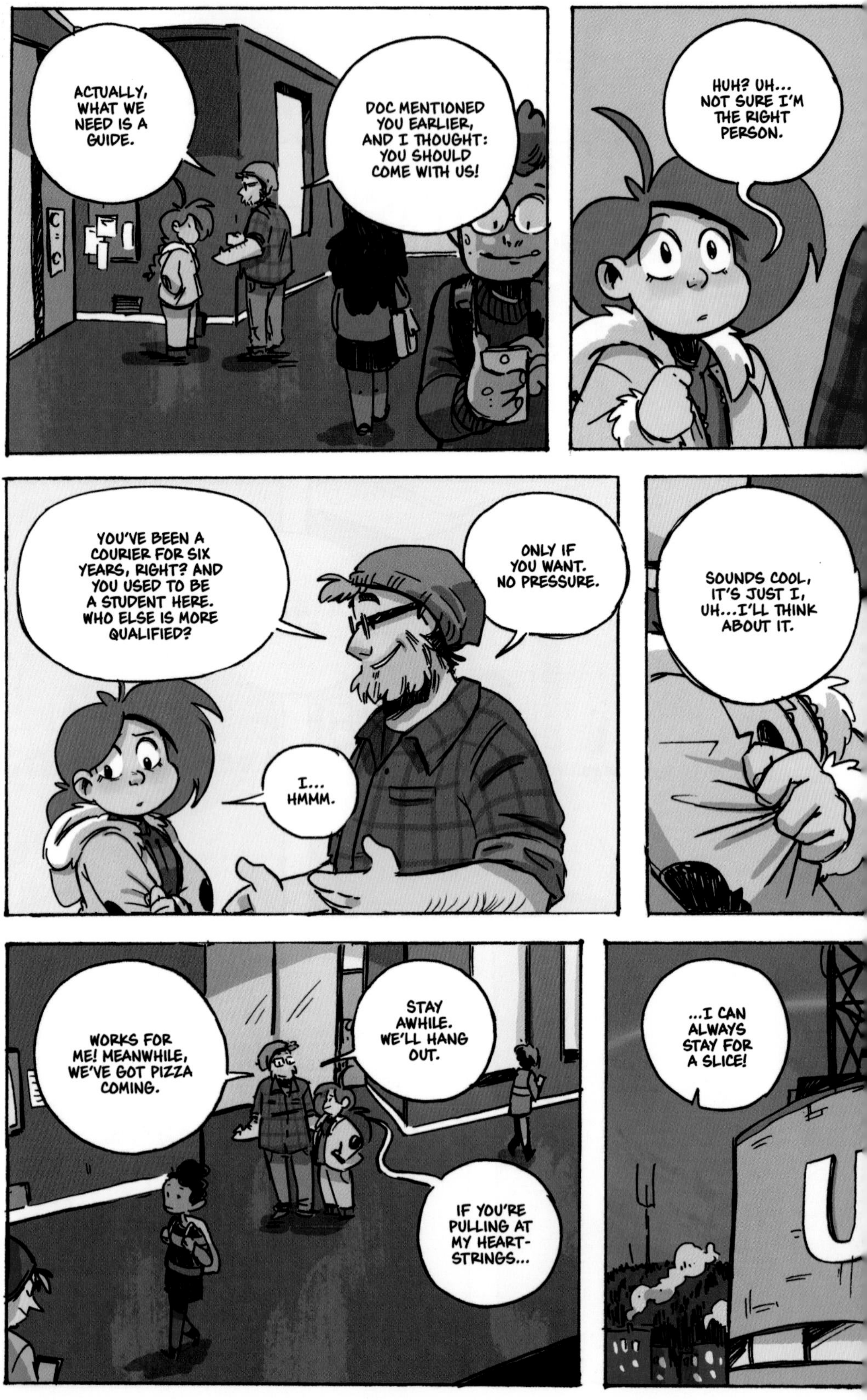
ACTUALLY, WHAT WE NEED IS A GUIDE.
DOC MENTIONED YOU EARLIER, AND I THOUGHT: YOU SHOULD COME WITH US!
HUH? UH... NOT SURE I'M THE RIGHT PERSON.
YOU'VE BEEN A COURIER FOR SIX YEARS, RIGHT? AND YOU USED TO BE A STUDENT HERE. WHO ELSE IS MORE QUALIFIED?
ONLY IF YOU WANT. NO PRESSURE.
I... HMMM.
SOUNDS COOL, IT'S JUST I, UH...I'LL THINK ABOUT IT.
WORKS FOR ME! MEANWHILE, WE'VE GOT PIZZA COMING.
STAY AWHILE. WE'LL HANG OUT.
IF YOU'RE PULLING AT MY HEART-STRINGS...
...I CAN ALWAYS STAY FOR A SLICE!
U

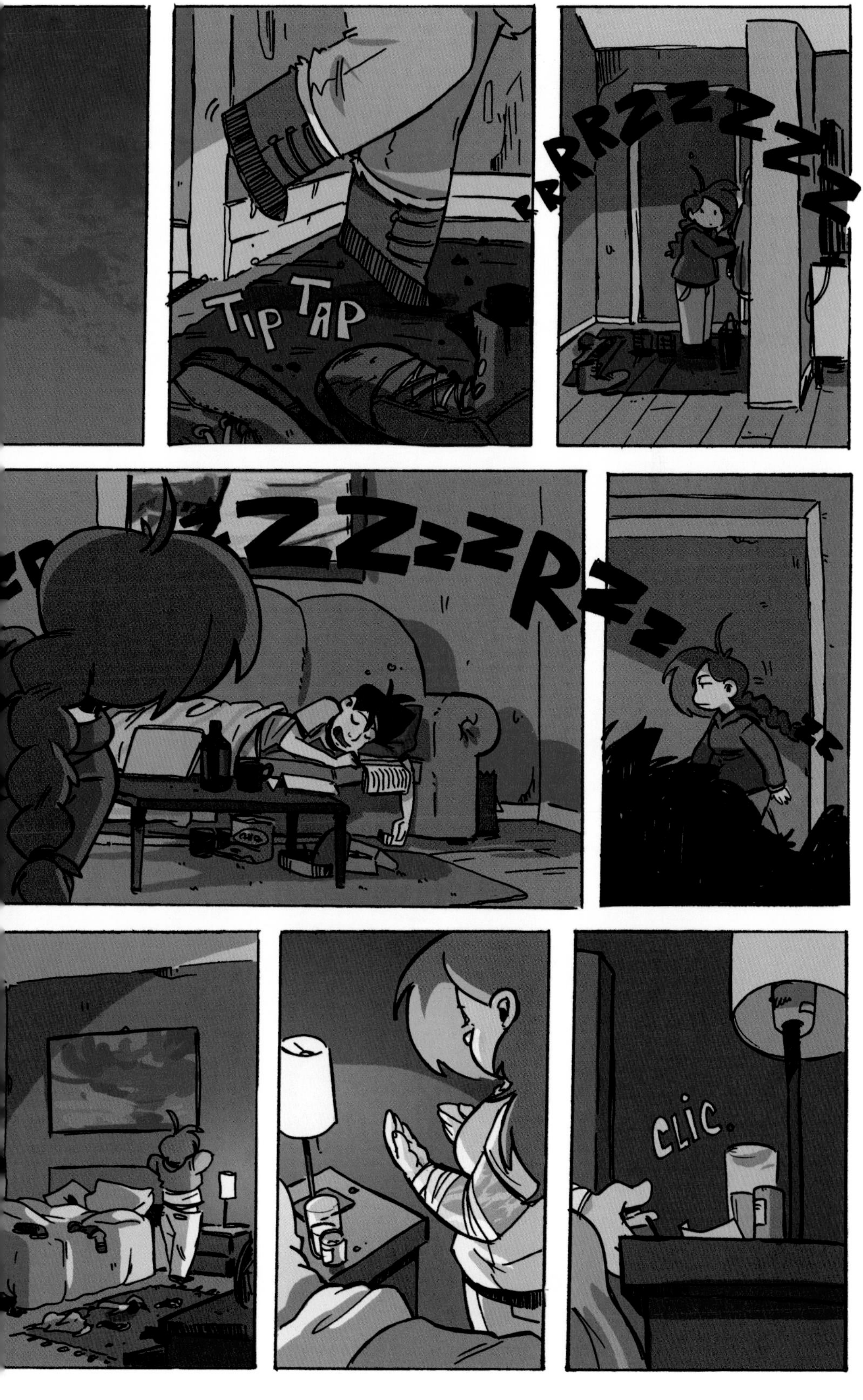
TIP TAP
CLIC.

CHAPTER 2
CLEAR SIGNALS

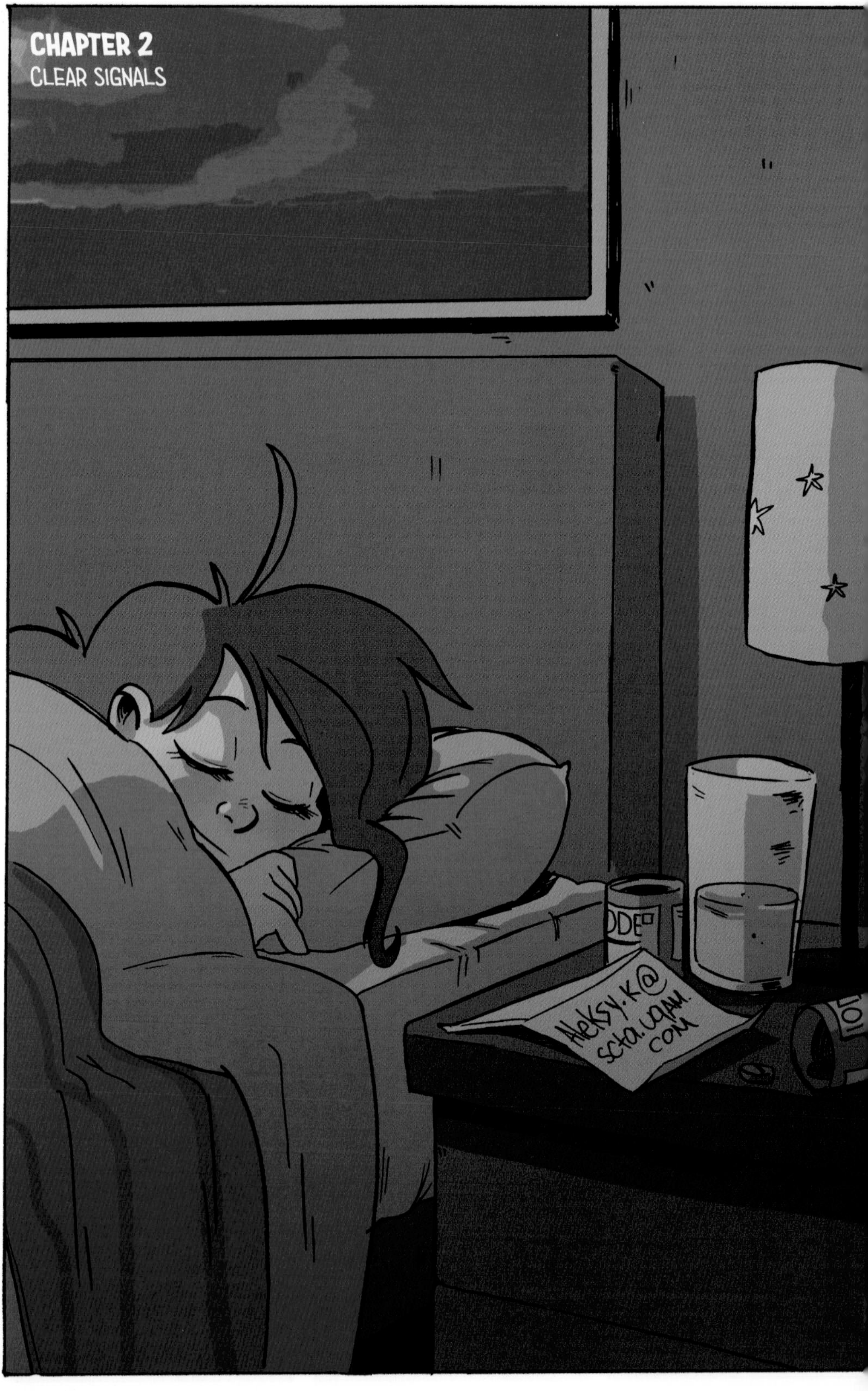
ALEKSY.K@
SCTA.UQAM.
COM

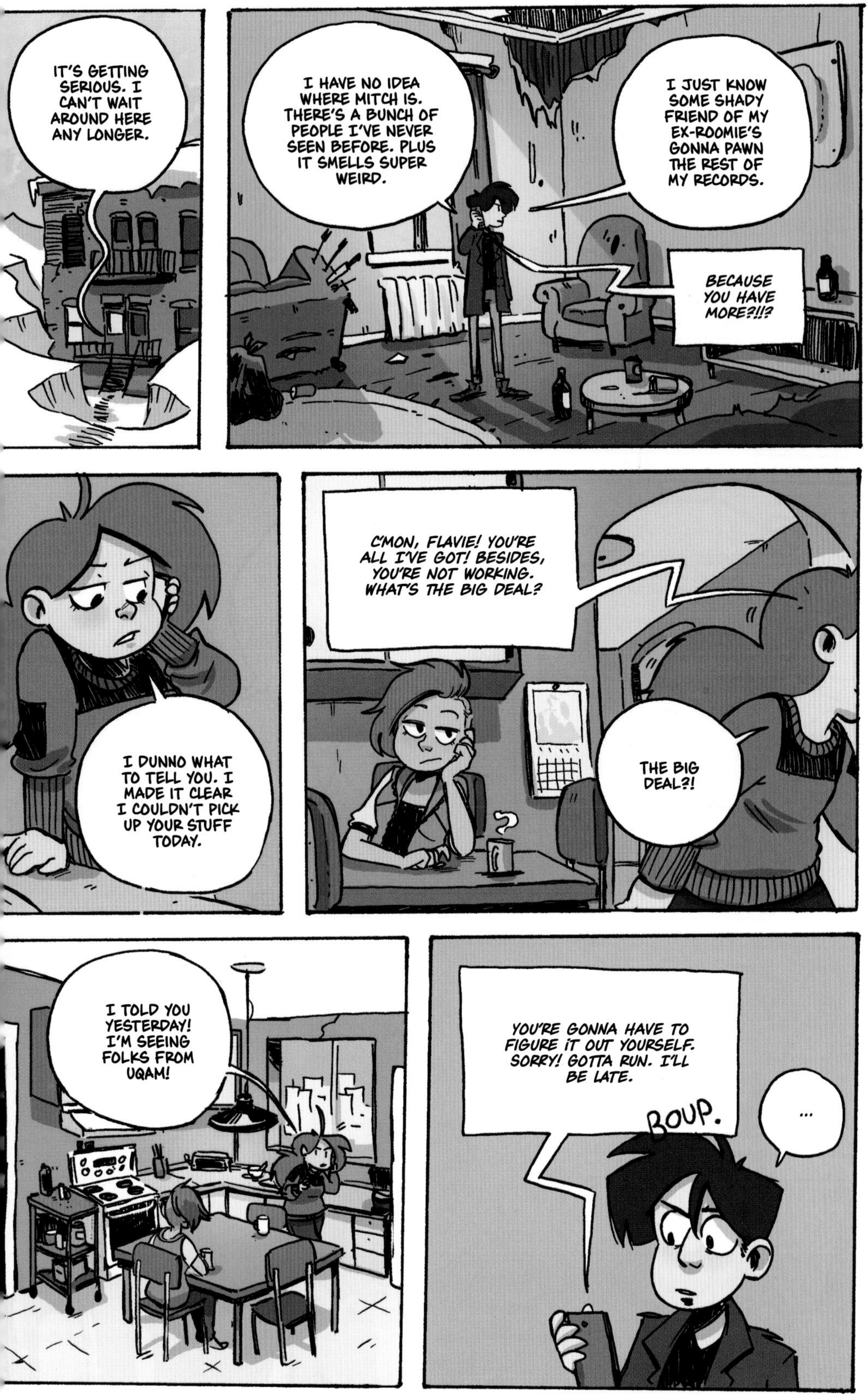
IT'S GETTING SERIOUS. I CAN'T WAIT AROUND HERE ANY LONGER.
I HAVE NO IDEA WHERE MITCH IS. THERE'S A BUNCH OF PEOPLE I'VE NEVER SEEN BEFORE. PLUS IT SMELLS SUPER WEIRD.
I JUST KNOW SOME SHADY FRIEND OF MY EX-ROOMIE'S GONNA PAWN THE REST OF MY RECORDS.
BECAUSE YOU HAVE MORE?!!?
I DUNNO WHAT TO TELL YOU. I MADE IT CLEAR I COULDN'T PICK UP YOUR STUFF TODAY.
C'MON, FLAVIE! YOU'RE ALL I'VE GOT! BESIDES, YOU'RE NOT WORKING. WHAT'S THE BIG DEAL?
THE BIG DEAL?!
I TOLD YOU YESTERDAY! I'M SEEING FOLKS FROM UQAM!
YOU'RE GONNA HAVE TO FIGURE IT OUT YOURSELF. SORRY! GOTTA RUN. I'LL BE LATE.
BOUP.
...

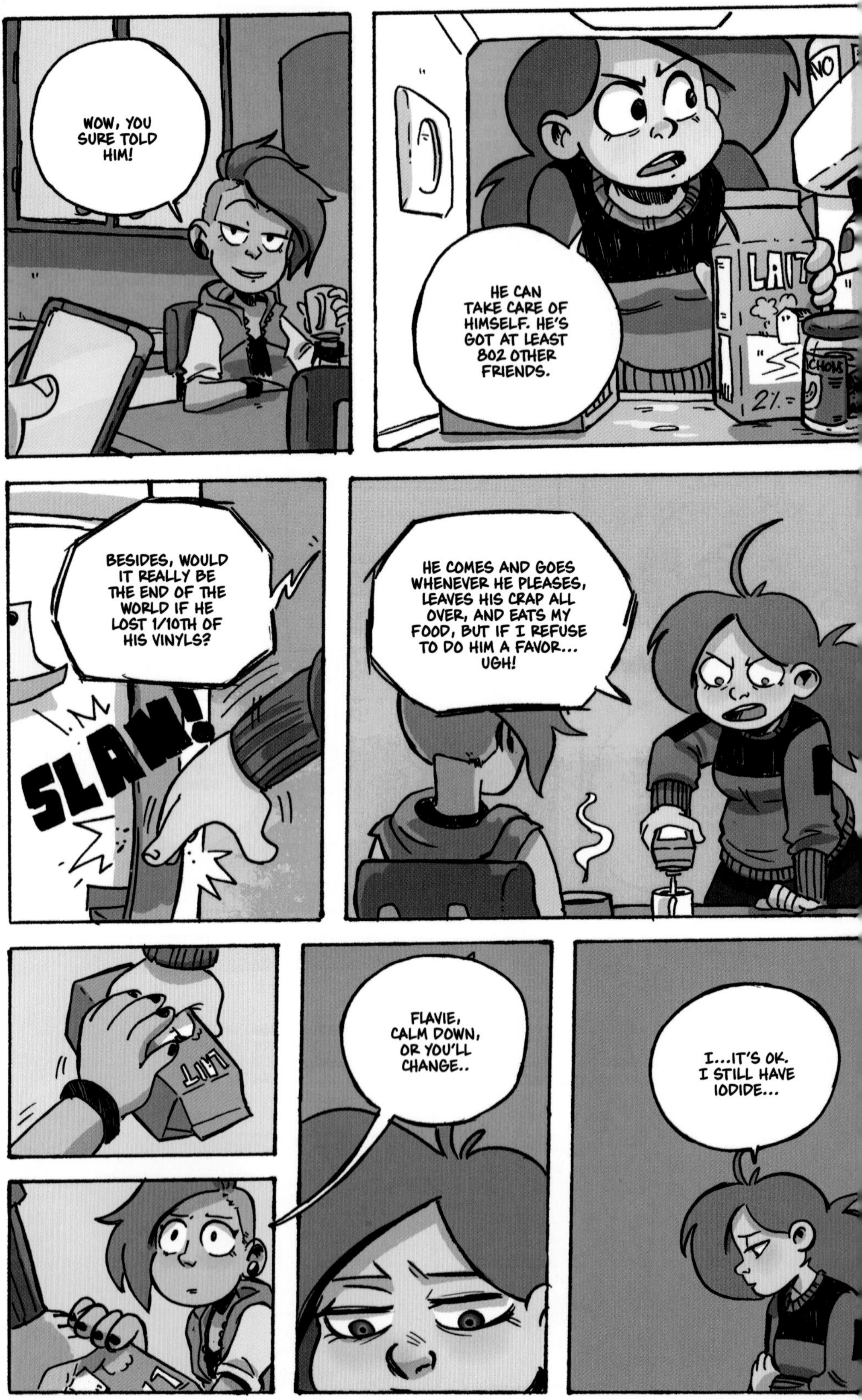
WOW, YOU SURE TOLD HIM!
NO
HE CAN TAKE CARE OF HIMSELF. HE'S GOT AT LEAST 802 OTHER FRIENDS.
LAIT
2%
BESIDES, WOULD IT REALLY BE THE END OF THE WORLD IF HE LOST 1/10TH OF HIS VINYLS?
SLAM!
HE COMES AND GOES WHENEVER HE PLEASES, LEAVES HIS CRAP ALL OVER, AND EATS MY FOOD, BUT IF I REFUSE TO DO HIM A FAVOR... UGH!
LAIT
FLAVIE, CALM DOWN, OR YOU'LL CHANGE..
I...IT'S OK. I STILL HAVE IODIDE...

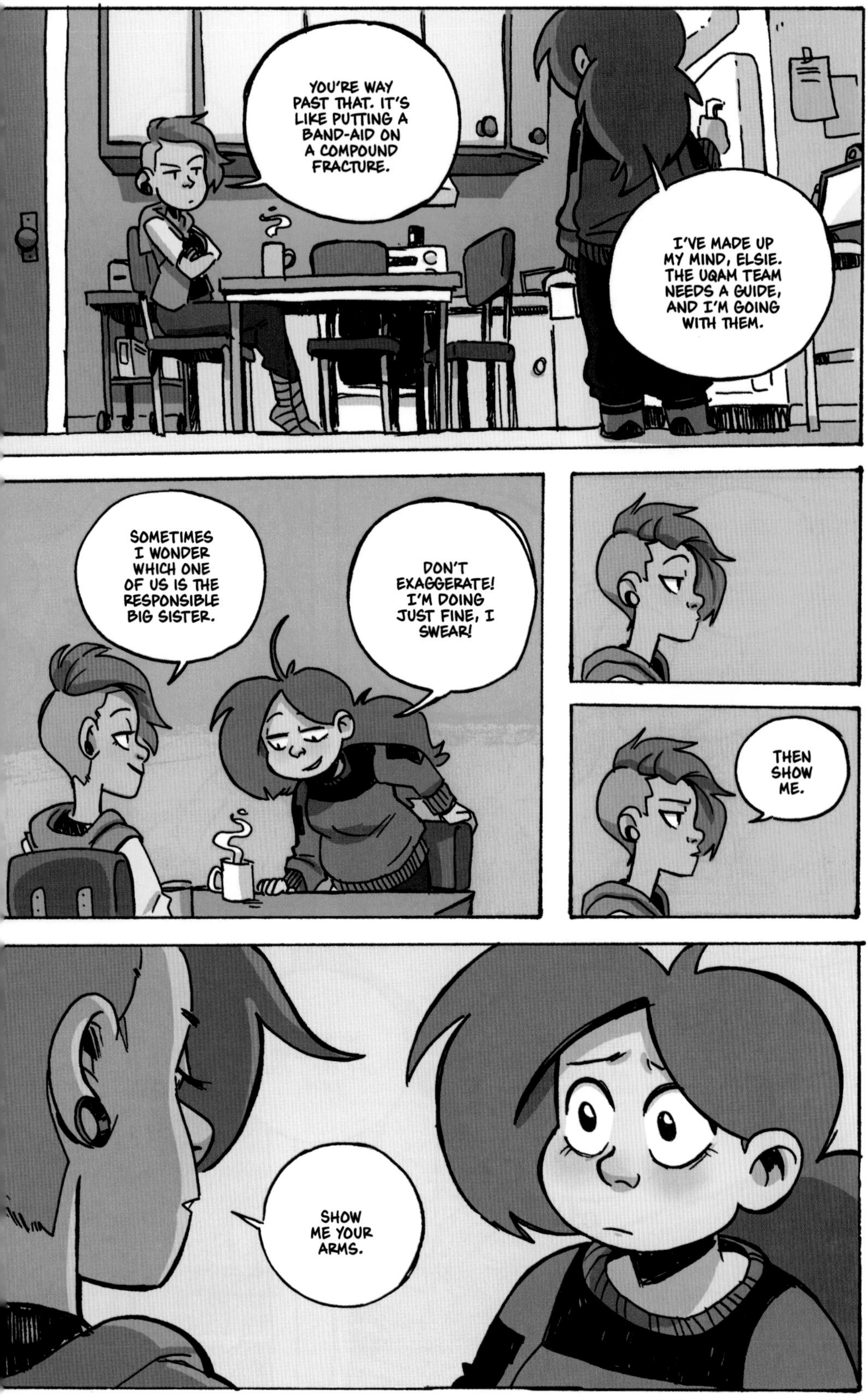
YOU'RE WAY PAST THAT. IT'S LIKE PUTTING A BAND-AID ON A COMPOUND FRACTURE.
I'VE MADE UP MY MIND, ELSIE. THE UQAM TEAM NEEDS A GUIDE, AND I'M GOING WITH THEM.
SOMETIMES I WONDER WHICH ONE OF US IS THE RESPONSIBLE BIG SISTER.
DON'T EXAGGERATE! I'M DOING JUST FINE, I SWEAR!
THEN SHOW ME.
SHOW ME YOUR ARMS.

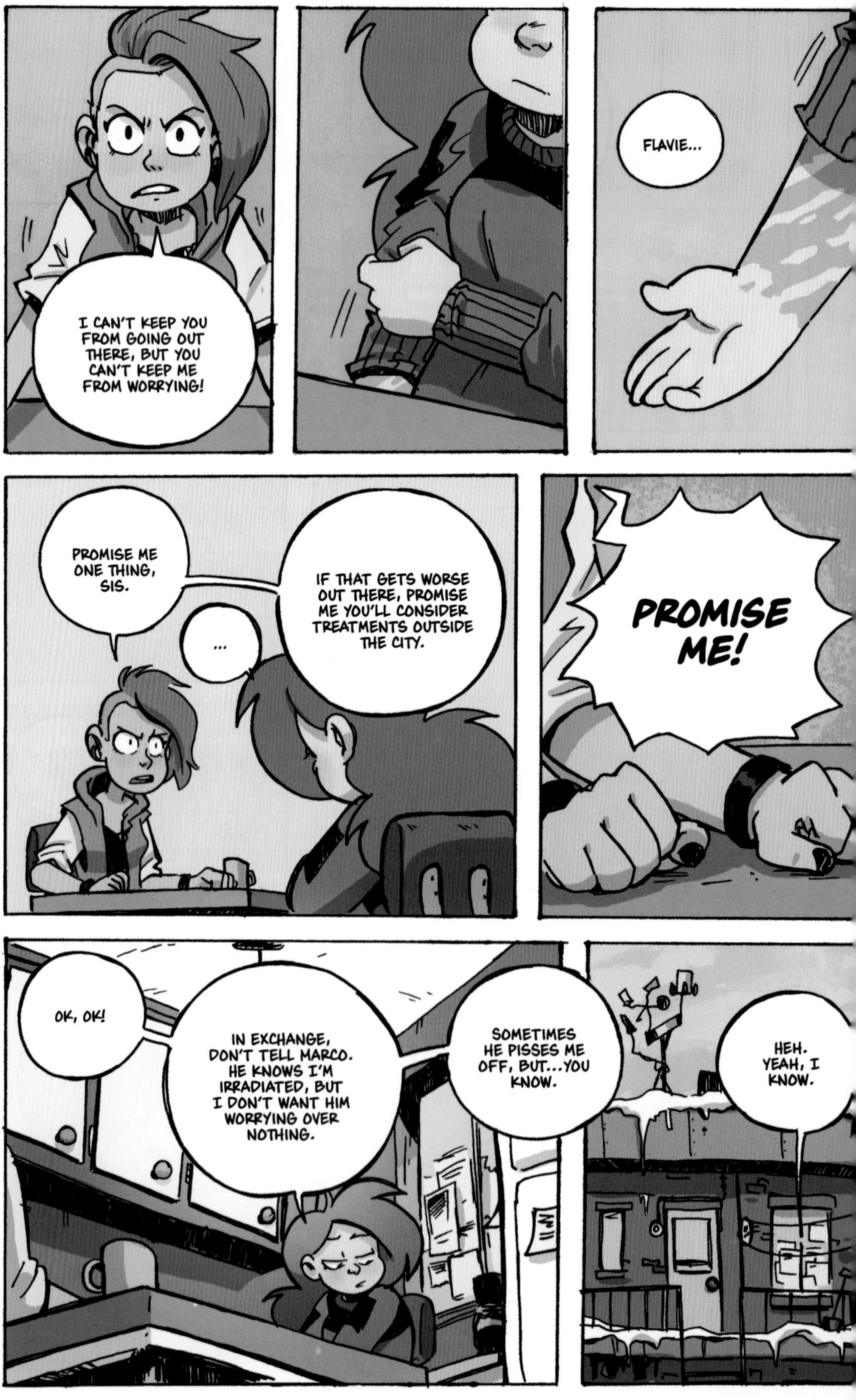
I CAN'T KEEP YOU FROM GOING OUT THERE, BUT YOU CAN'T KEEP ME FROM WORRYING!
FLAVIE...
PROMISE ME ONE THING, SIS.
IF THAT GETS WORSE OUT THERE, PROMISE ME YOU'LL CONSIDER TREATMENTS OUTSIDE THE CITY.
...
PROMISE ME!
OK, OK!
IN EXCHANGE, DON'T TELL MARCO. HE KNOWS I'M IRRADIATED, BUT I DON'T WANT HIM WORRYING OVER NOTHING.
SOMETIMES HE PISSES ME OFF, BUT...YOU KNOW.
HEH. YEAH, I KNOW.

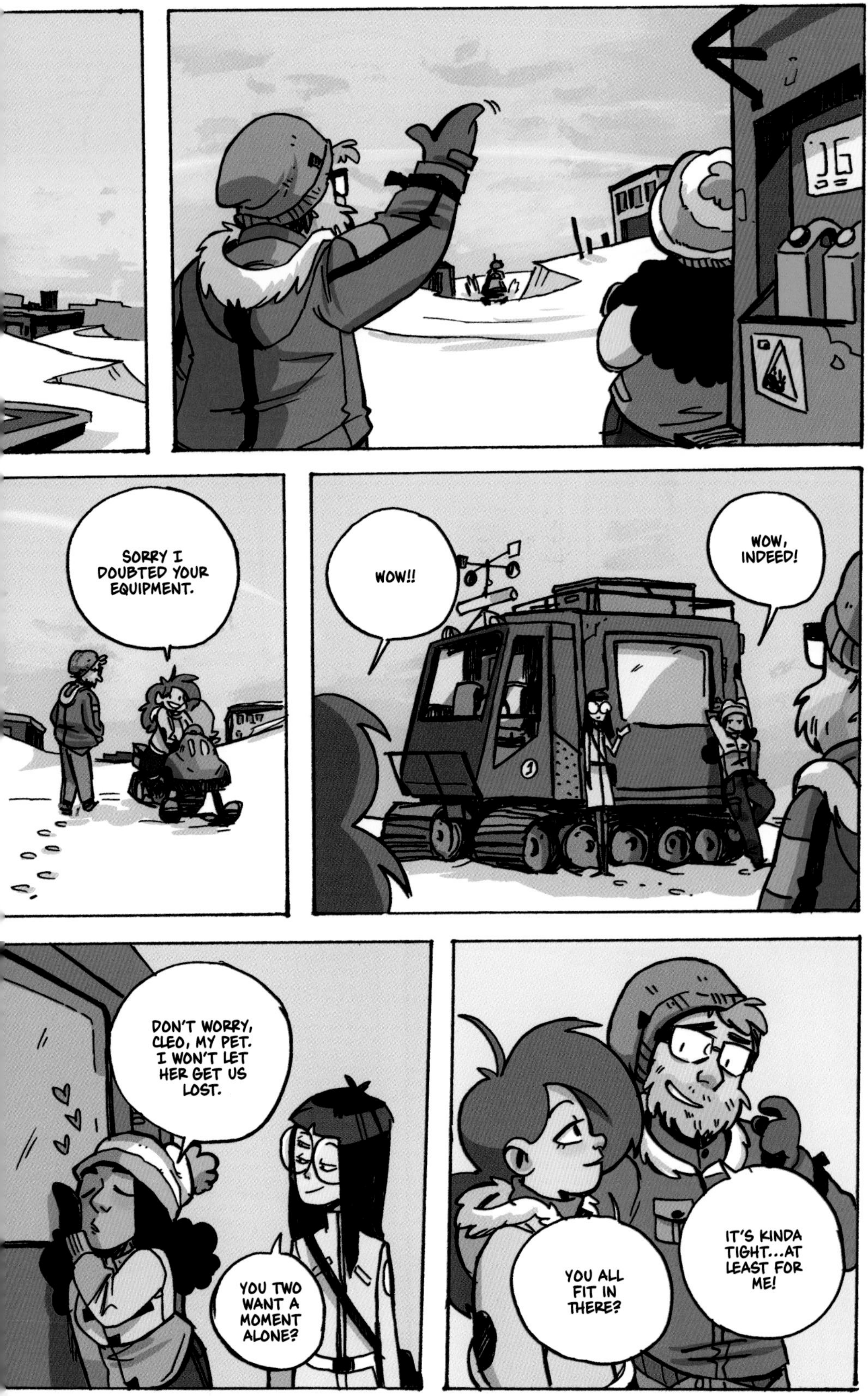
SORRY I DOUBTED YOUR EQUIPMENT.
WOW!!
WOW, INDEED!
DON'T WORRY, CLEO, MY PET. I WON'T LET HER GET US LOST.
YOU TWO WANT A MOMENT ALONE?
YOU ALL FIT IN THERE?
IT'S KINDA TIGHT...AT LEAST FOR ME!

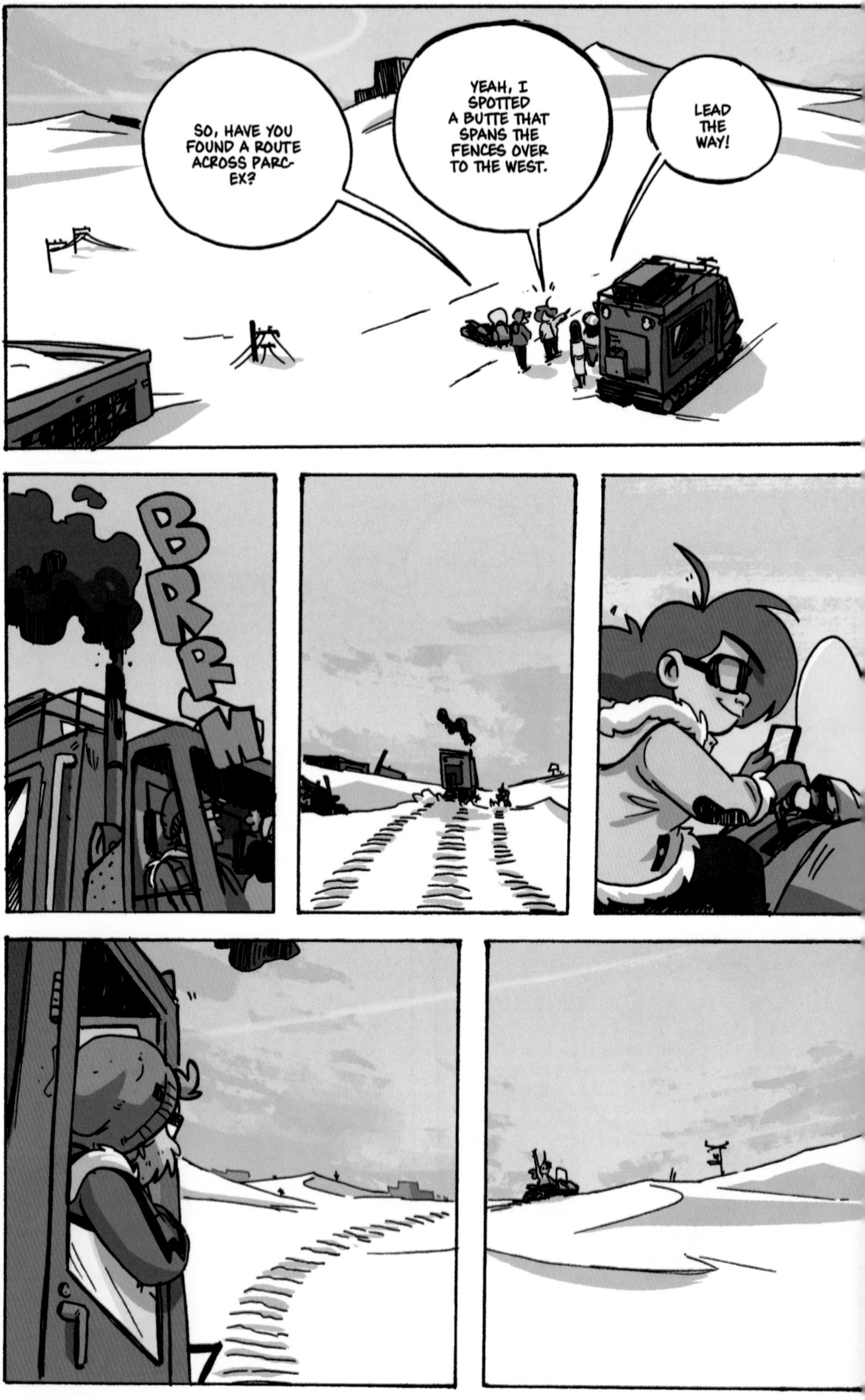
SO, HAVE YOU FOUND A ROUTE ACROSS PARC-EX?
YEAH, I SPOTTED A BUTTE THAT SPANS THE FENCES OVER TO THE WEST.
LEAD THE WAY!
BRRRM

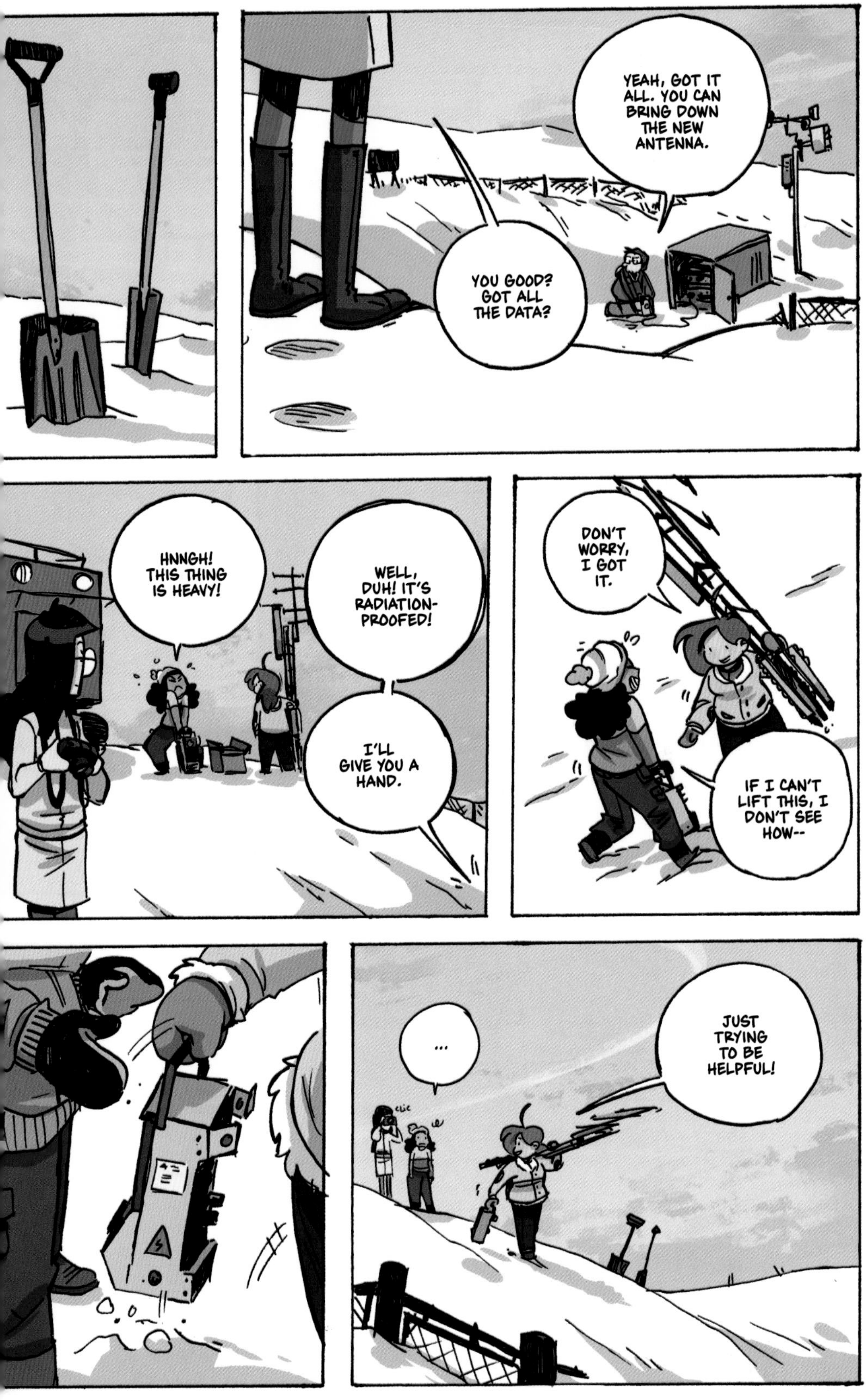
YEAH, GOT IT ALL. YOU CAN BRING DOWN THE NEW ANTENNA.
YOU GOOD? GOT ALL THE DATA?
HNNGH! THIS THING IS HEAVY!
WELL, DUH! IT'S RADIATION-PROOFED!
I'LL GIVE YOU A HAND.
DON'T WORRY, I GOT IT.
IF I CAN'T LIFT THIS, I DON'T SEE HOW--
...
JUST TRYING TO BE HELPFUL!

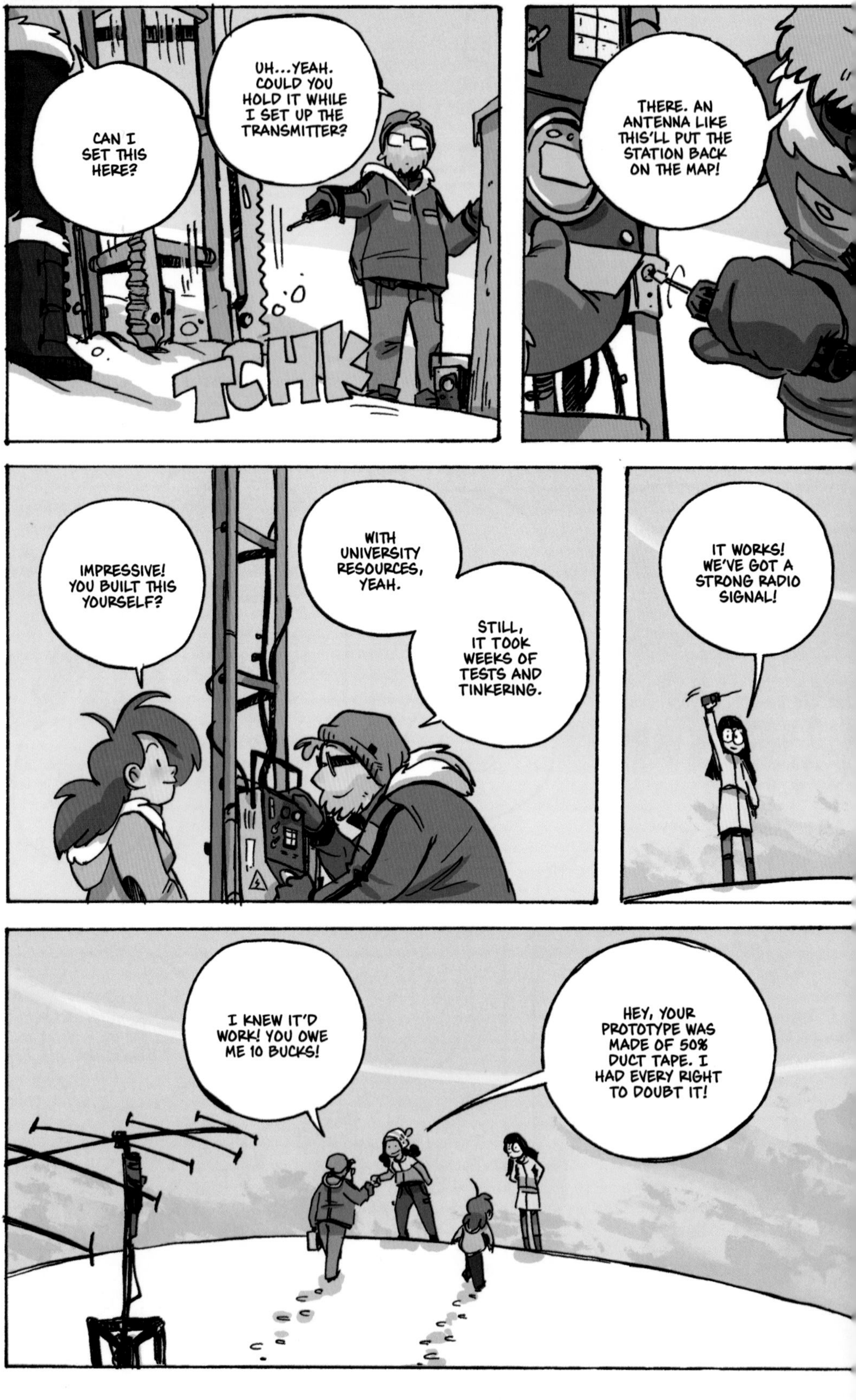
CAN I SET THIS HERE?
UH...YEAH. COULD YOU HOLD IT WHILE I SET UP THE TRANSMITTER?
TCHK
THERE. AN ANTENNA LIKE THIS'LL PUT THE STATION BACK ON THE MAP!
IMPRESSIVE! YOU BUILT THIS YOURSELF?
WITH UNIVERSITY RESOURCES, YEAH.
STILL, IT TOOK WEEKS OF TESTS AND TINKERING.
IT WORKS! WE'VE GOT A STRONG RADIO SIGNAL!
I KNEW IT'D WORK! YOU OWE ME 10 BUCKS!
HEY, YOUR PROTOTYPE WAS MADE OF 50% DUCT TAPE. I HAD EVERY RIGHT TO DOUBT IT!

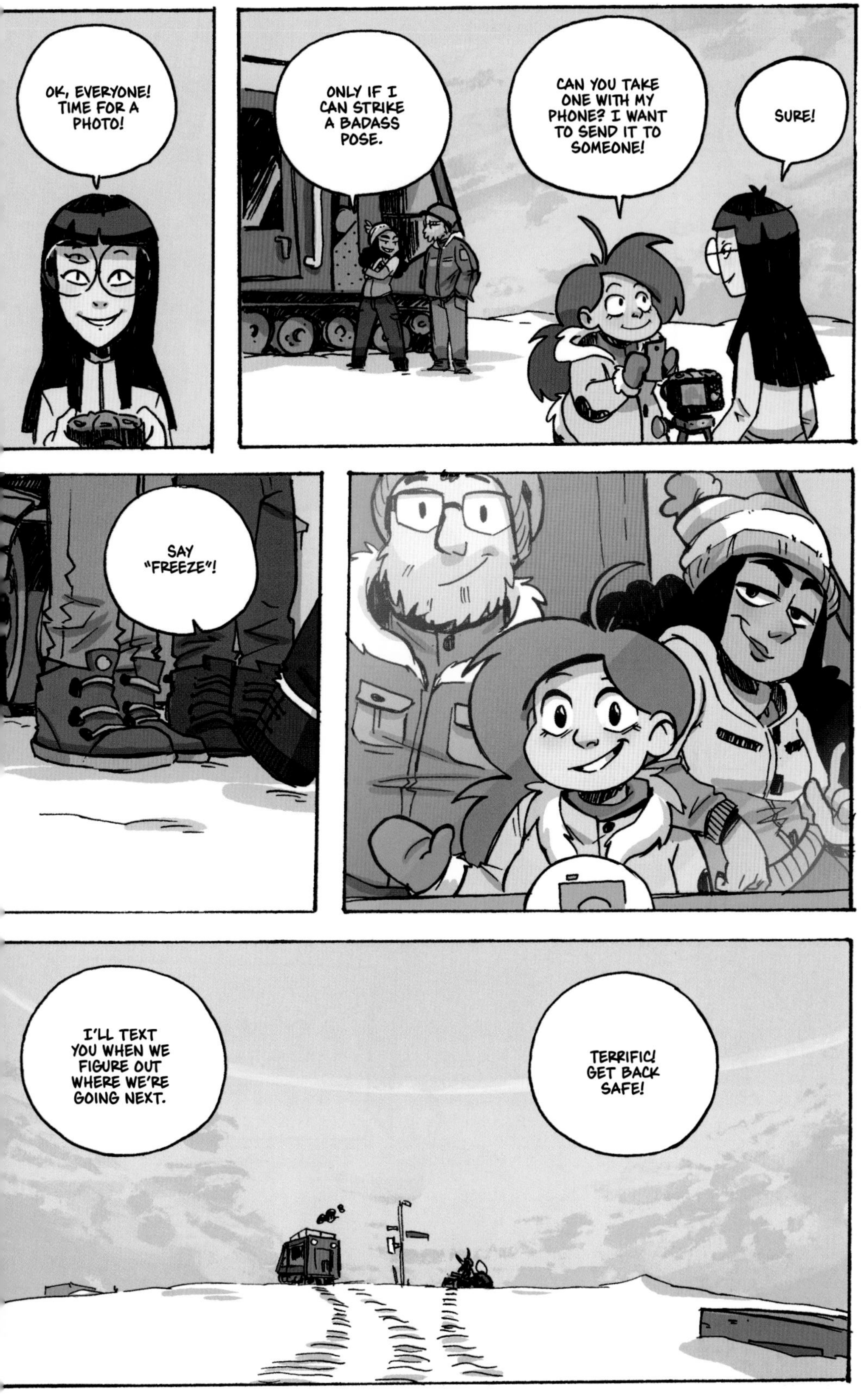
OK, EVERYONE! TIME FOR A PHOTO!
ONLY IF I CAN STRIKE A BADASS POSE.
CAN YOU TAKE ONE WITH MY PHONE? I WANT TO SEND IT TO SOMEONE!
SURE!
SAY "FREEZE"!
I'LL TEXT YOU WHEN WE FIGURE OUT WHERE WE'RE GOING NEXT.
TERRIFIC! GET BACK SAFE!

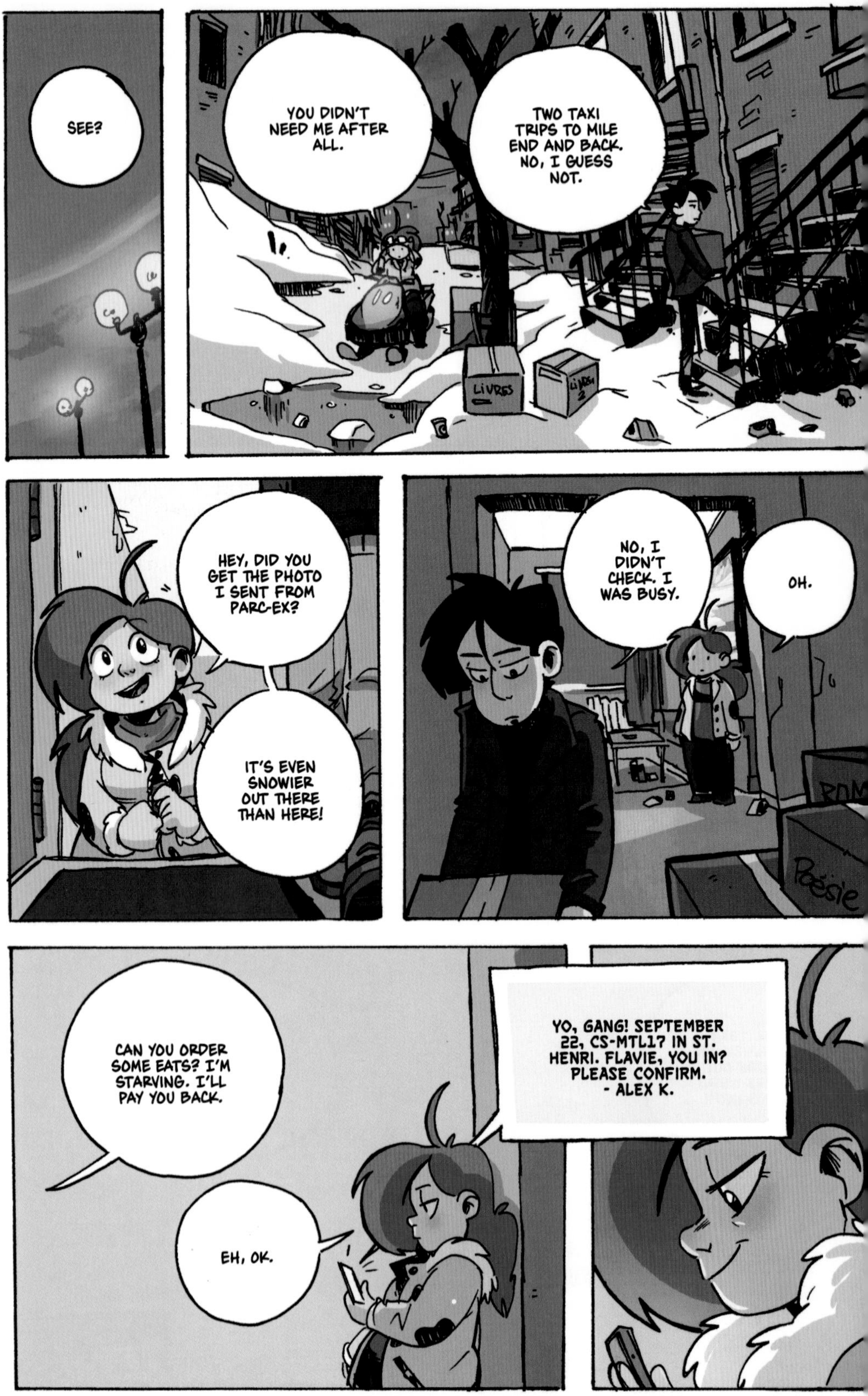
SEE?
YOU DIDN'T NEED ME AFTER ALL.
TWO TAXI TRIPS TO MILE END AND BACK. NO, I GUESS NOT.
LIVRES
HEY, DID YOU GET THE PHOTO I SENT FROM PARC-EX?
IT'S EVEN SNOWIER OUT THERE THAN HERE!
NO, I DIDN'T CHECK. I WAS BUSY.
OH.
Poésie
CAN YOU ORDER SOME EATS? I'M STARVING. I'LL PAY YOU BACK.
EH, OK.
YO, GANG! SEPTEMBER 22, CS-MTL17 IN ST. HENRI. FLAVIE, YOU IN? PLEASE CONFIRM. - ALEX K.

OK, HOLD IT STEADY. WE'RE GOOD.

YO, FLAVIE! QUIT TAKING PHOTOS. WE HAVE TO GET TO THE OTHER STATION BEFORE NIGHTFALL!

COMING!

I KNOW A SHORTCUT, BUT I DON'T KNOW IF YOU CAN MAKE IT THROUGH.

PSHAW! I BET WE'LL BEAT YOU THERE IF YOU TELL US WHERE TO GO.

YOU REALLY WANT TO RACE A COURIER?

OH, DON'T UNDERESTIMATE CLEO AND HER DRIVER!

LESS TALK, MORE SPEED!

C'MON, ALEX! OUR TRUCK ISN'T A RACE CAR!

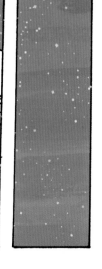

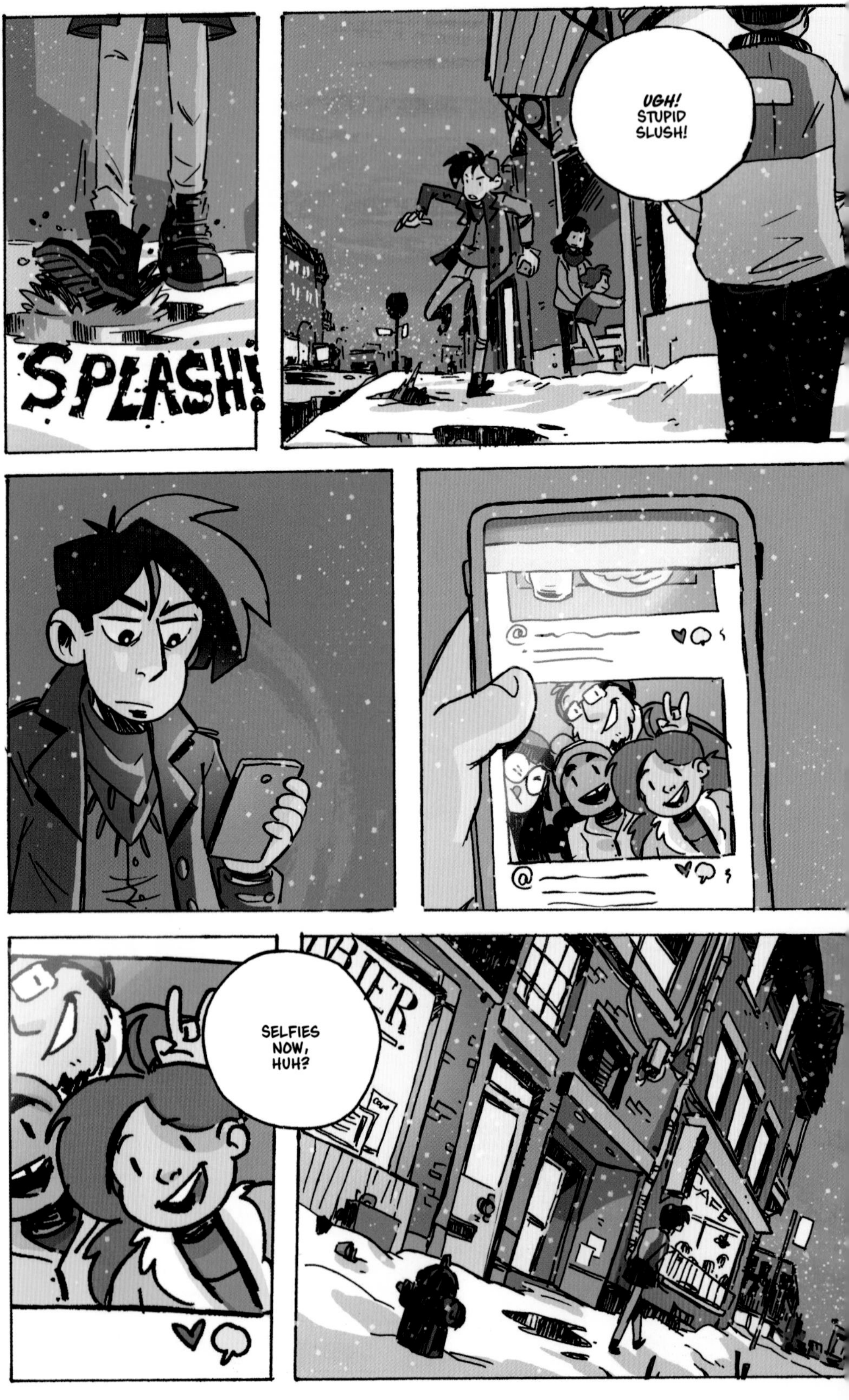
SPLASH!
UGH! STUPID SLUSH!
SELFIES NOW, HUH?

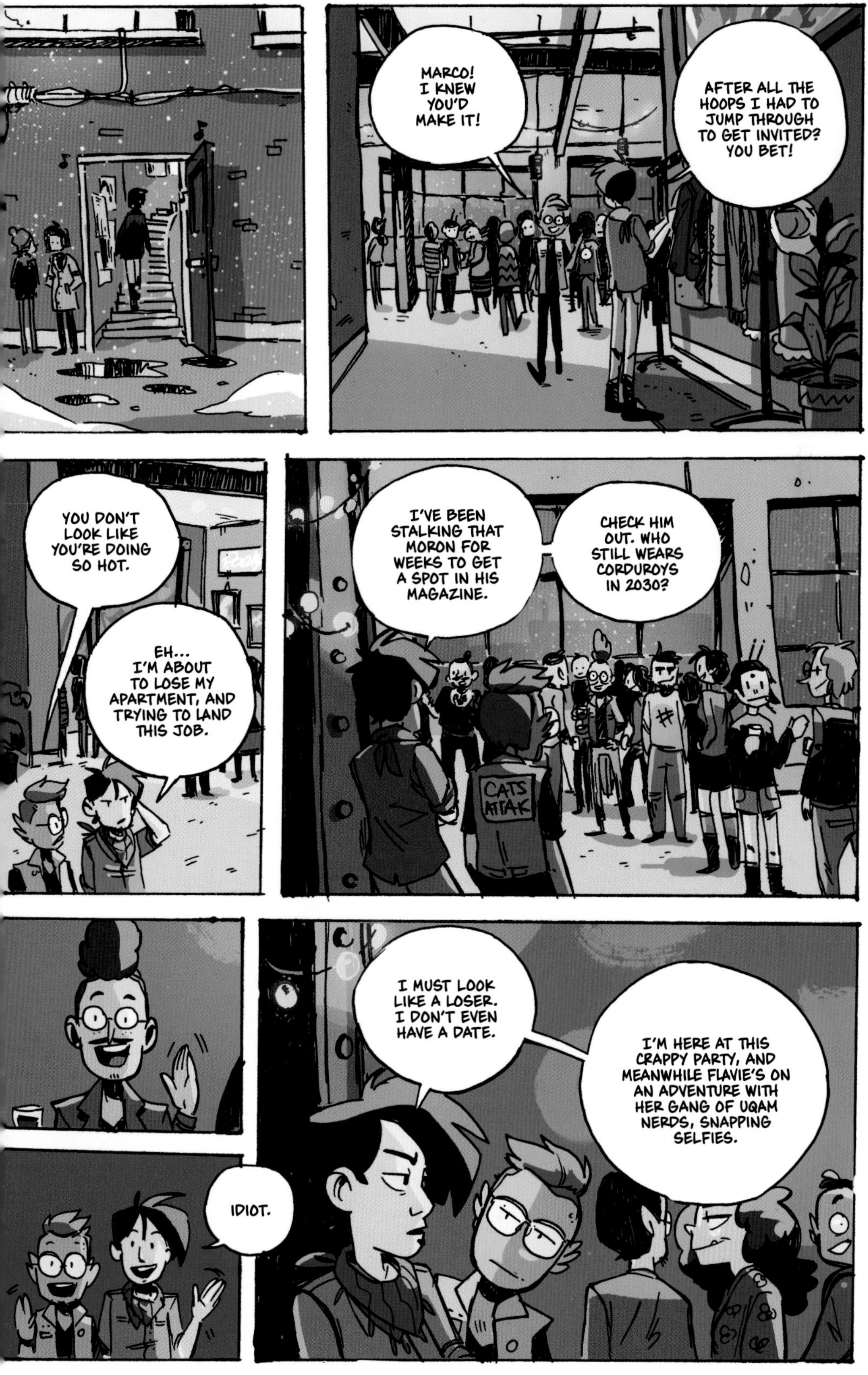
MARCO! I KNEW YOU'D MAKE IT!
AFTER ALL THE HOOPS I HAD TO JUMP THROUGH TO GET INVITED? YOU BET!
YOU DON'T LOOK LIKE YOU'RE DOING SO HOT.
EH... I'M ABOUT TO LOSE MY APARTMENT, AND TRYING TO LAND THIS JOB.
I'VE BEEN STALKING THAT MORON FOR WEEKS TO GET A SPOT IN HIS MAGAZINE.
CHECK HIM OUT. WHO STILL WEARS CORDUROYS IN 2030?
CATS ATTAK
I MUST LOOK LIKE A LOSER. I DON'T EVEN HAVE A DATE.
I'M HERE AT THIS CRAPPY PARTY, AND MEANWHILE FLAVIE'S ON AN ADVENTURE WITH HER GANG OF UQAM NERDS, SNAPPING SELFIES.
IDIOT.

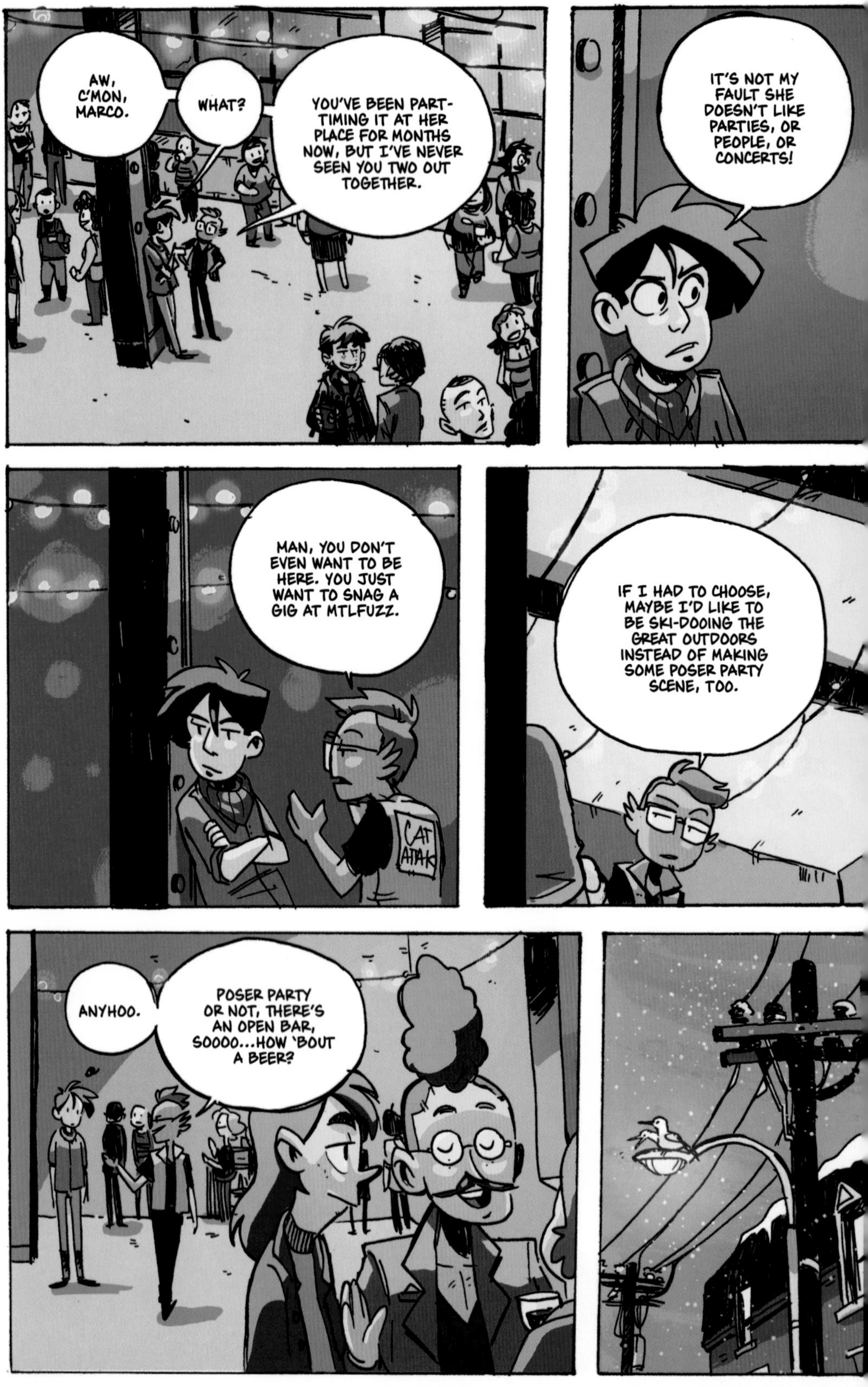
AW, C'MON, MARCO.
WHAT?
YOU'VE BEEN PART-TIMING IT AT HER PLACE FOR MONTHS NOW, BUT I'VE NEVER SEEN YOU TWO OUT TOGETHER.
IT'S NOT MY FAULT SHE DOESN'T LIKE PARTIES, OR PEOPLE, OR CONCERTS!
MAN, YOU DON'T EVEN WANT TO BE HERE. YOU JUST WANT TO SNAG A GIG AT MTLFUZZ.
CAT ATTAK
IF I HAD TO CHOOSE, MAYBE I'D LIKE TO BE SKI-DOOING THE GREAT OUTDOORS INSTEAD OF MAKING SOME POSER PARTY SCENE, TOO.
ANYHOO.
POSER PARTY OR NOT, THERE'S AN OPEN BAR, SOOOO...HOW 'BOUT A BEER?

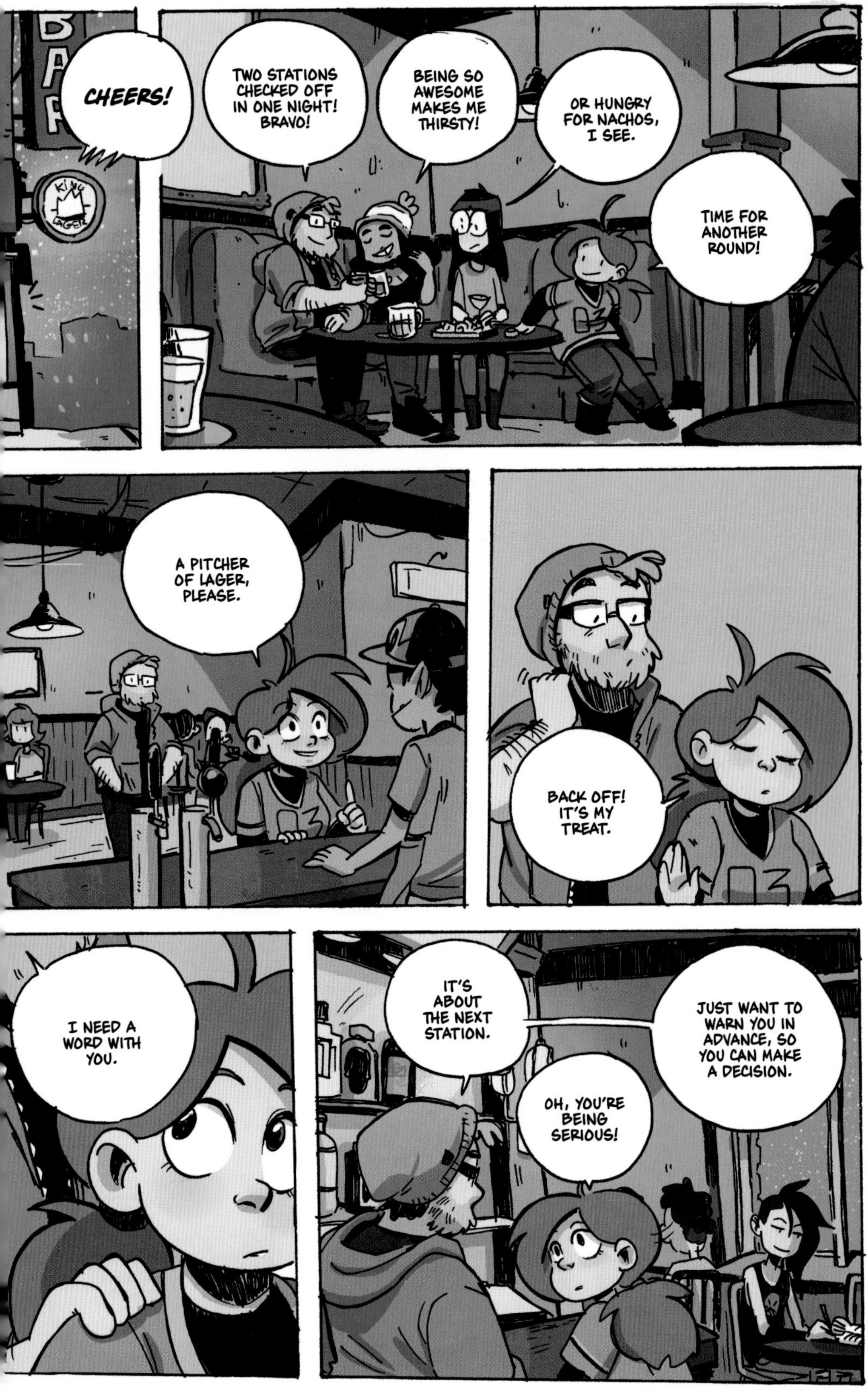

BAR
KING LAGER
CHEERS!
TWO STATIONS CHECKED OFF IN ONE NIGHT! BRAVO!
BEING SO AWESOME MAKES ME THIRSTY!
OR HUNGRY FOR NACHOS, I SEE.
TIME FOR ANOTHER ROUND!
A PITCHER OF LAGER, PLEASE.
BACK OFF! IT'S MY TREAT.
I NEED A WORD WITH YOU.
IT'S ABOUT THE NEXT STATION.
JUST WANT TO WARN YOU IN ADVANCE, SO YOU CAN MAKE A DECISION.
OH, YOU'RE BEING SERIOUS!

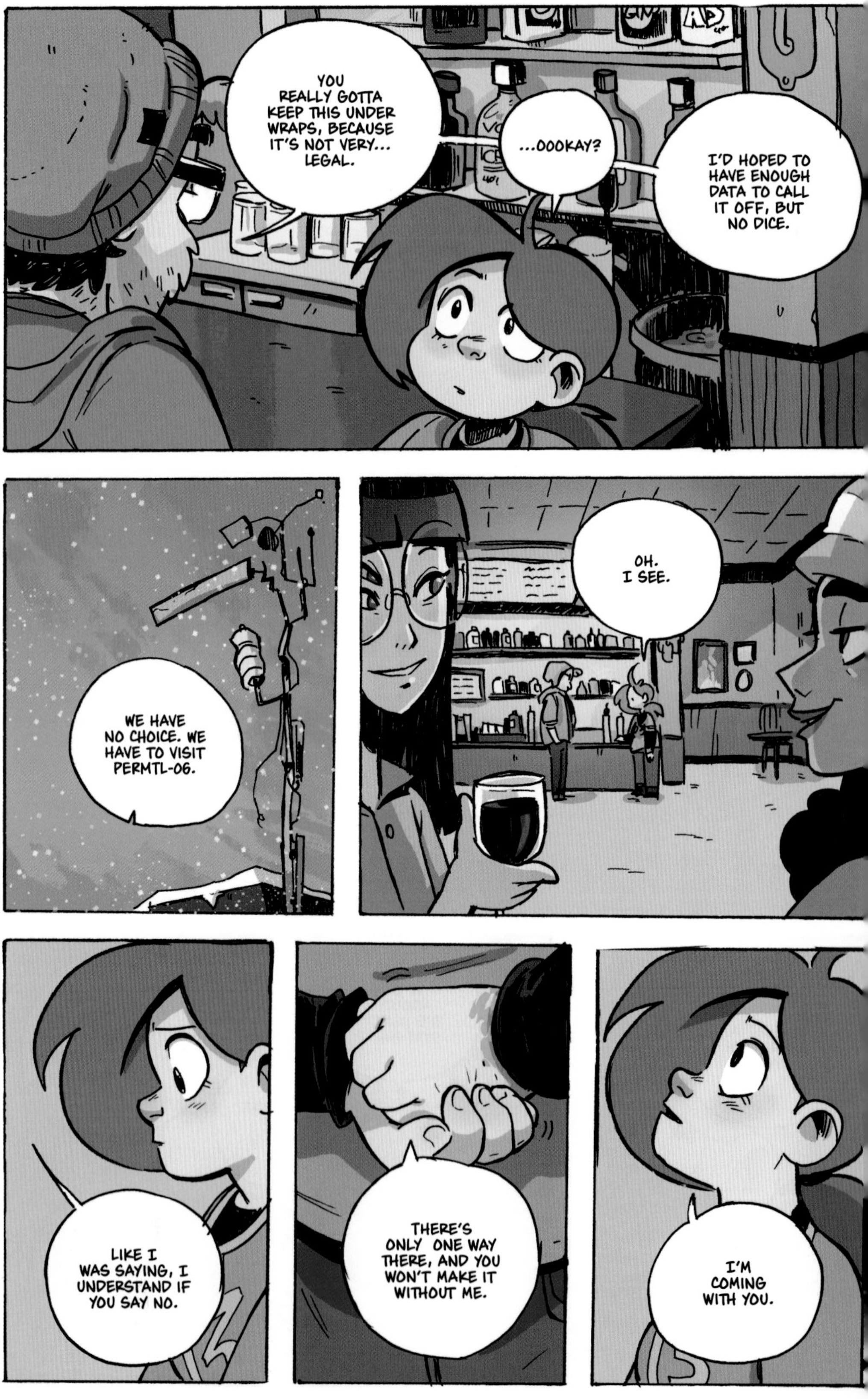
YOU REALLY GOTTA KEEP THIS UNDER WRAPS, BECAUSE IT'S NOT VERY... LEGAL.
...OOOKAY?
I'D HOPED TO HAVE ENOUGH DATA TO CALL IT OFF, BUT NO DICE.
WE HAVE NO CHOICE. WE HAVE TO VISIT PERMTL-06.
OH. I SEE.
LIKE I WAS SAYING, I UNDERSTAND IF YOU SAY NO.
THERE'S ONLY ONE WAY THERE, AND YOU WON'T MAKE IT WITHOUT ME.
I'M COMING WITH YOU.

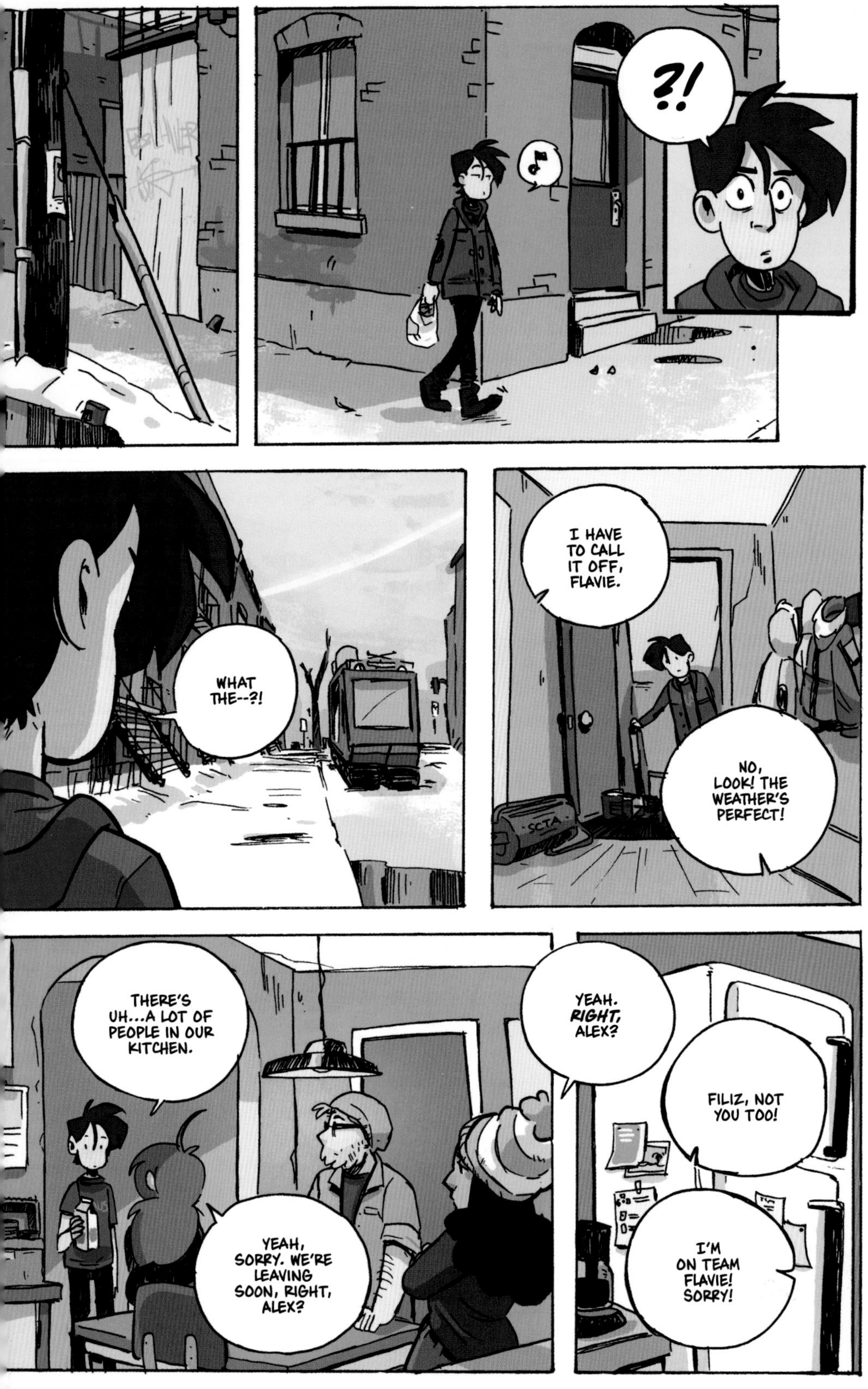

?!
WHAT THE--?!
I HAVE TO CALL IT OFF, FLAVIE.
NO, LOOK! THE WEATHER'S PERFECT!
SCTA
THERE'S UH...A LOT OF PEOPLE IN OUR KITCHEN.
YEAH, SORRY. WE'RE LEAVING SOON, RIGHT, ALEX?
YEAH. *RIGHT*, ALEX?
FILIZ, NOT YOU TOO!
I'M ON TEAM FLAVIE! SORRY!

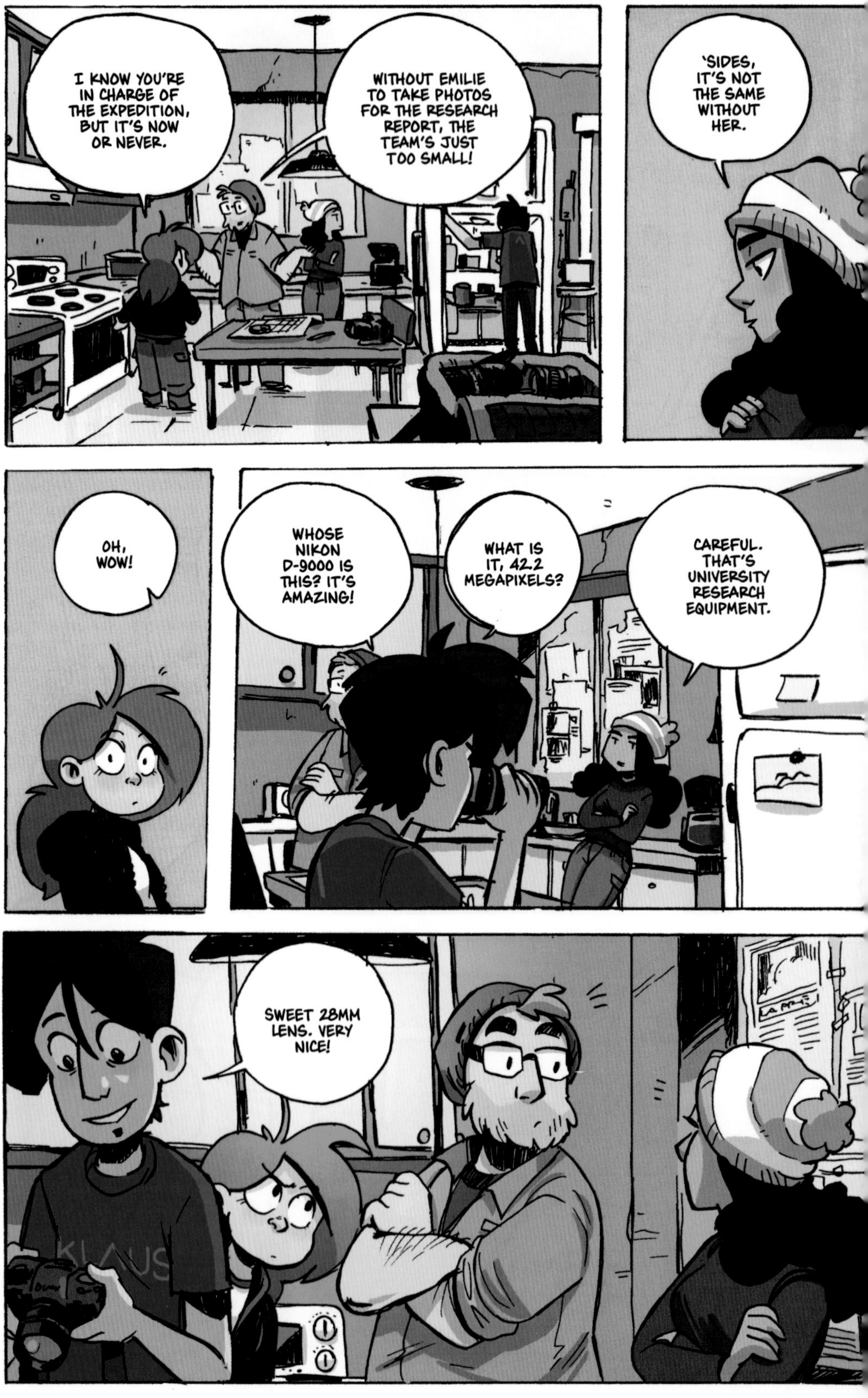
I KNOW YOU'RE IN CHARGE OF THE EXPEDITION, BUT IT'S NOW OR NEVER.
WITHOUT EMILIE TO TAKE PHOTOS FOR THE RESEARCH REPORT, THE TEAM'S JUST TOO SMALL!
'SIDES, IT'S NOT THE SAME WITHOUT HER.
OH, WOW!
WHOSE NIKON D-9000 IS THIS? IT'S AMAZING!
WHAT IS IT, 42.2 MEGAPIXELS?
CAREFUL. THAT'S UNIVERSITY RESEARCH EQUIPMENT.
SWEET 28MM LENS. VERY NICE!
KLAUS

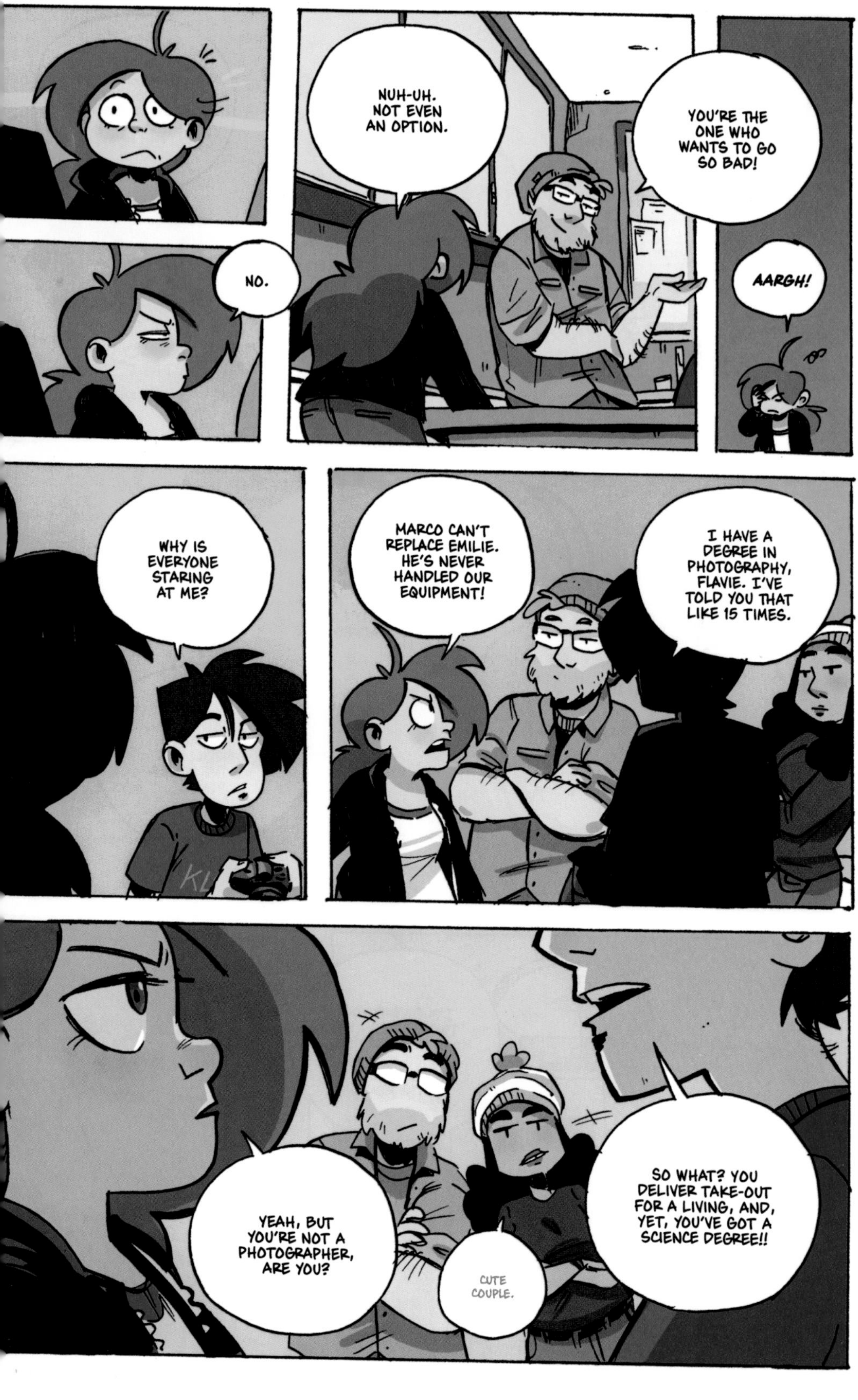
NO.
NUH-UH. NOT EVEN AN OPTION.
YOU'RE THE ONE WHO WANTS TO GO SO BAD!
AARGH!
WHY IS EVERYONE STARING AT ME?
MARCO CAN'T REPLACE EMILIE. HE'S NEVER HANDLED OUR EQUIPMENT!
I HAVE A DEGREE IN PHOTOGRAPHY, FLAVIE. I'VE TOLD YOU THAT LIKE 15 TIMES.
YEAH, BUT YOU'RE NOT A PHOTOGRAPHER, ARE YOU?
CUTE COUPLE.
SO WHAT? YOU DELIVER TAKE-OUT FOR A LIVING, AND, YET, YOU'VE GOT A SCIENCE DEGREE!!

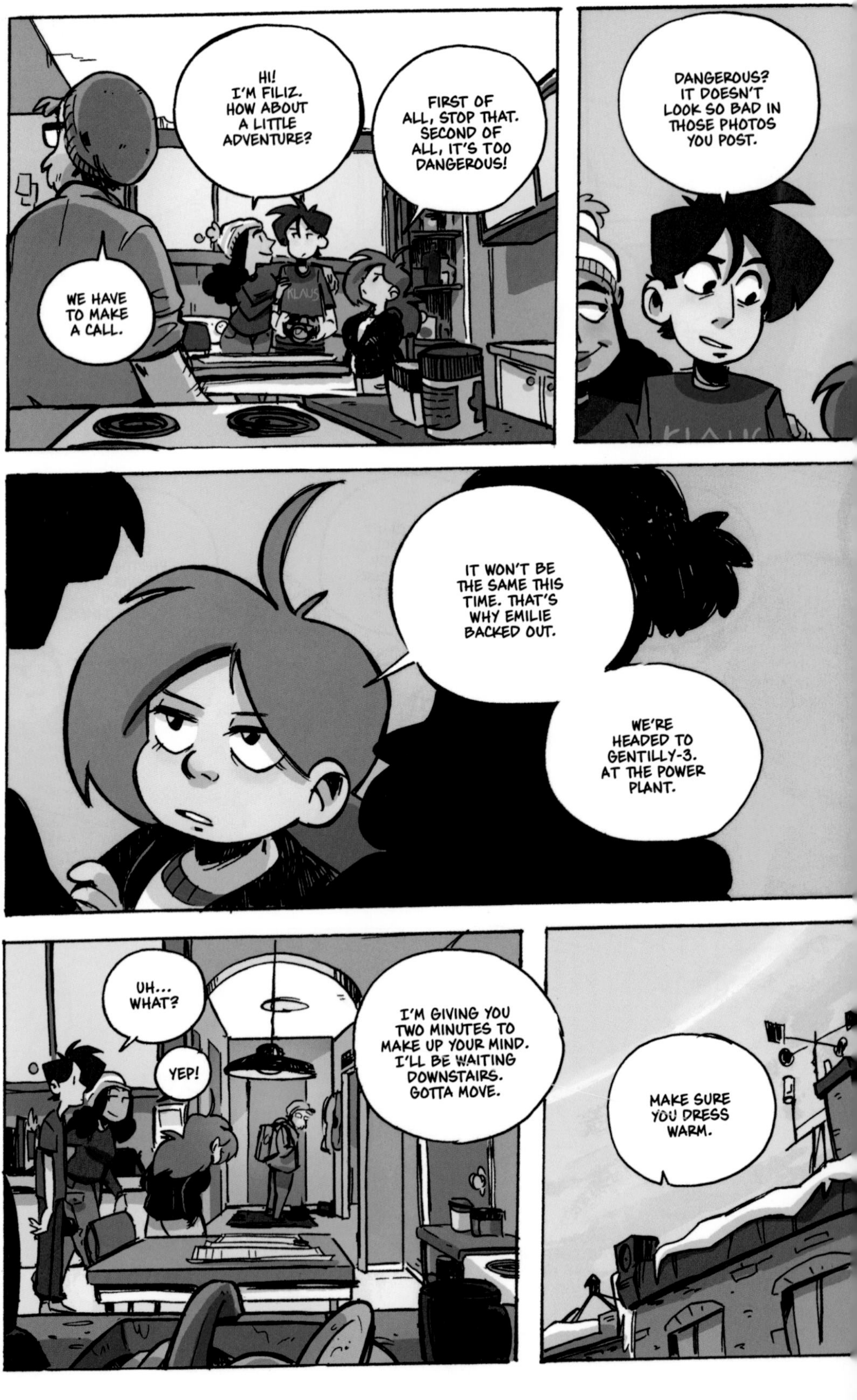
HI!
I'M FILIZ. HOW ABOUT A LITTLE ADVENTURE?
FIRST OF ALL, STOP THAT. SECOND OF ALL, IT'S TOO DANGEROUS!
WE HAVE TO MAKE A CALL.
KLAUS
DANGEROUS? IT DOESN'T LOOK SO BAD IN THOSE PHOTOS YOU POST.
IT WON'T BE THE SAME THIS TIME. THAT'S WHY EMILIE BACKED OUT.
WE'RE HEADED TO GENTILLY-3. AT THE POWER PLANT.
UH... WHAT?
YEP!
I'M GIVING YOU TWO MINUTES TO MAKE UP YOUR MIND. I'LL BE WAITING DOWNSTAIRS. GOTTA MOVE.
MAKE SURE YOU DRESS WARM.

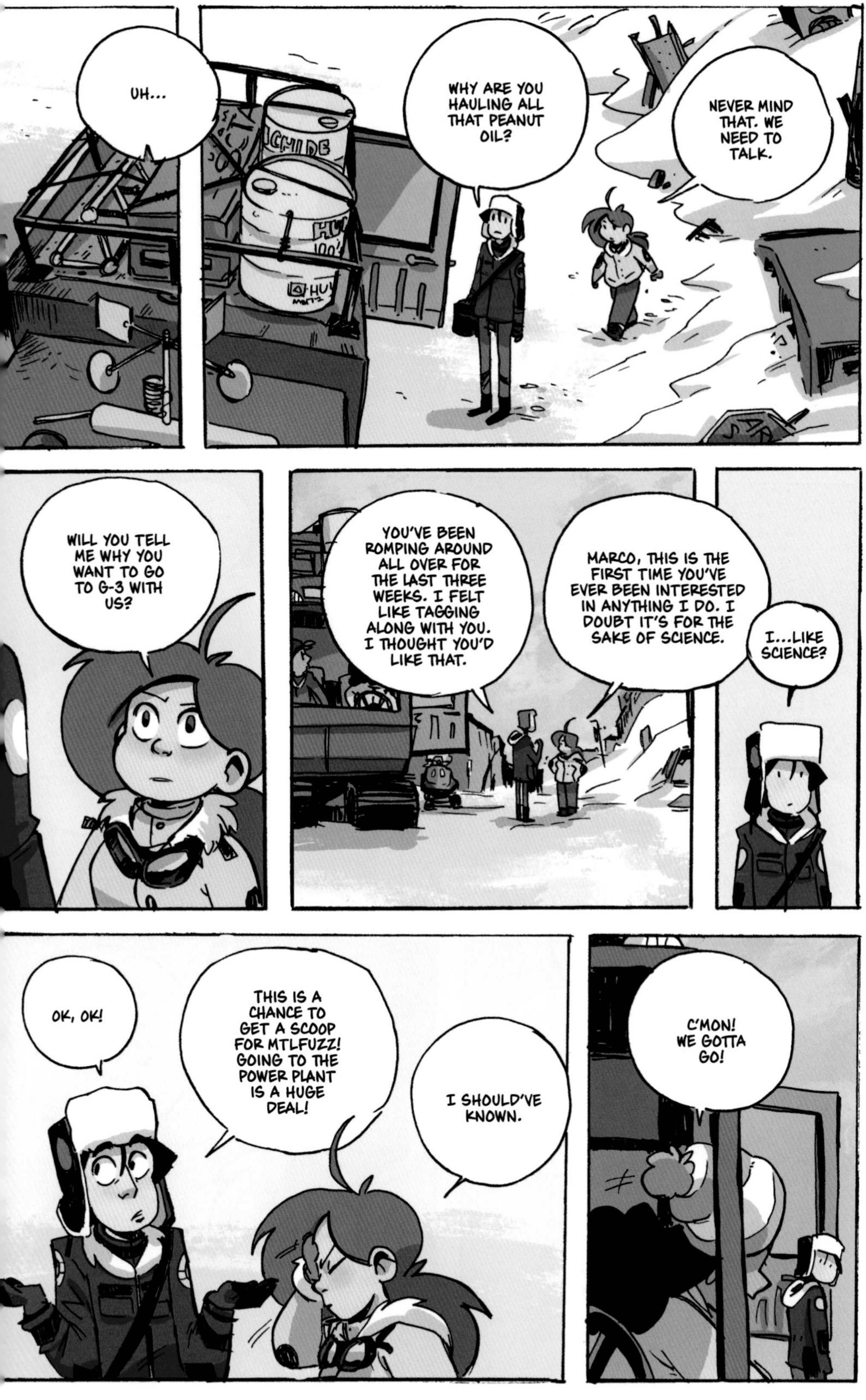
UH...
WHY ARE YOU HAULING ALL THAT PEANUT OIL?
NEVER MIND THAT. WE NEED TO TALK.
WILL YOU TELL ME WHY YOU WANT TO GO TO G-3 WITH US?
YOU'VE BEEN ROMPING AROUND ALL OVER FOR THE LAST THREE WEEKS. I FELT LIKE TAGGING ALONG WITH YOU. I THOUGHT YOU'D LIKE THAT.
MARCO, THIS IS THE FIRST TIME YOU'VE EVER BEEN INTERESTED IN ANYTHING I DO. I DOUBT IT'S FOR THE SAKE OF SCIENCE.
I...LIKE SCIENCE?
OK, OK!
THIS IS A CHANCE TO GET A SCOOP FOR MTLFUZZ! GOING TO THE POWER PLANT IS A HUGE DEAL!
I SHOULD'VE KNOWN.
C'MON! WE GOTTA GO!

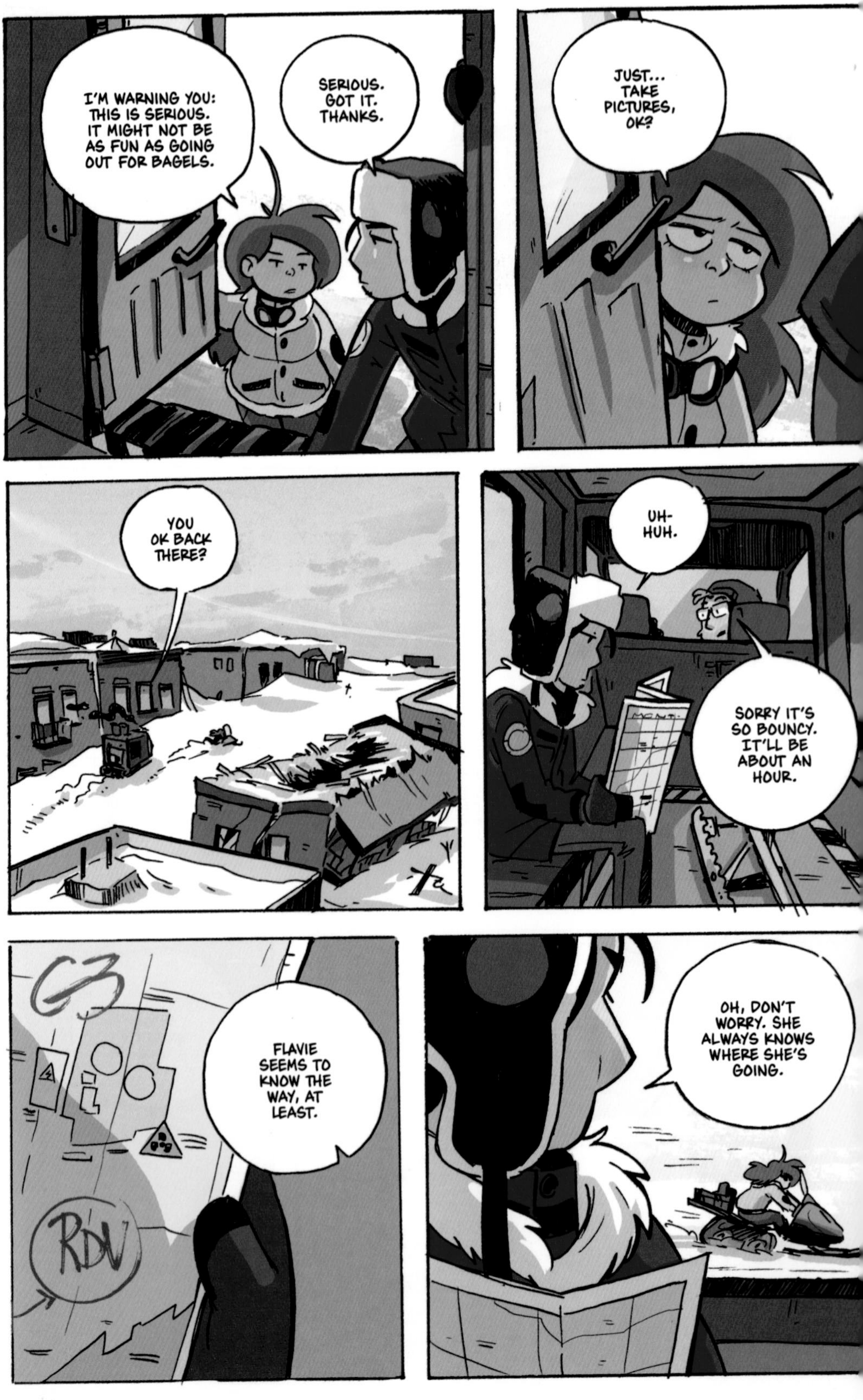
I'M WARNING YOU: THIS IS SERIOUS. IT MIGHT NOT BE AS FUN AS GOING OUT FOR BAGELS.
SERIOUS. GOT IT. THANKS.
JUST... TAKE PICTURES, OK?
YOU OK BACK THERE?
UH-HUH.
SORRY IT'S SO BOUNCY. IT'LL BE ABOUT AN HOUR.
FLAVIE SEEMS TO KNOW THE WAY, AT LEAST.
RDV
OH, DON'T WORRY. SHE ALWAYS KNOWS WHERE SHE'S GOING.

CHAPTER 3
THE FREE TERRITORIES

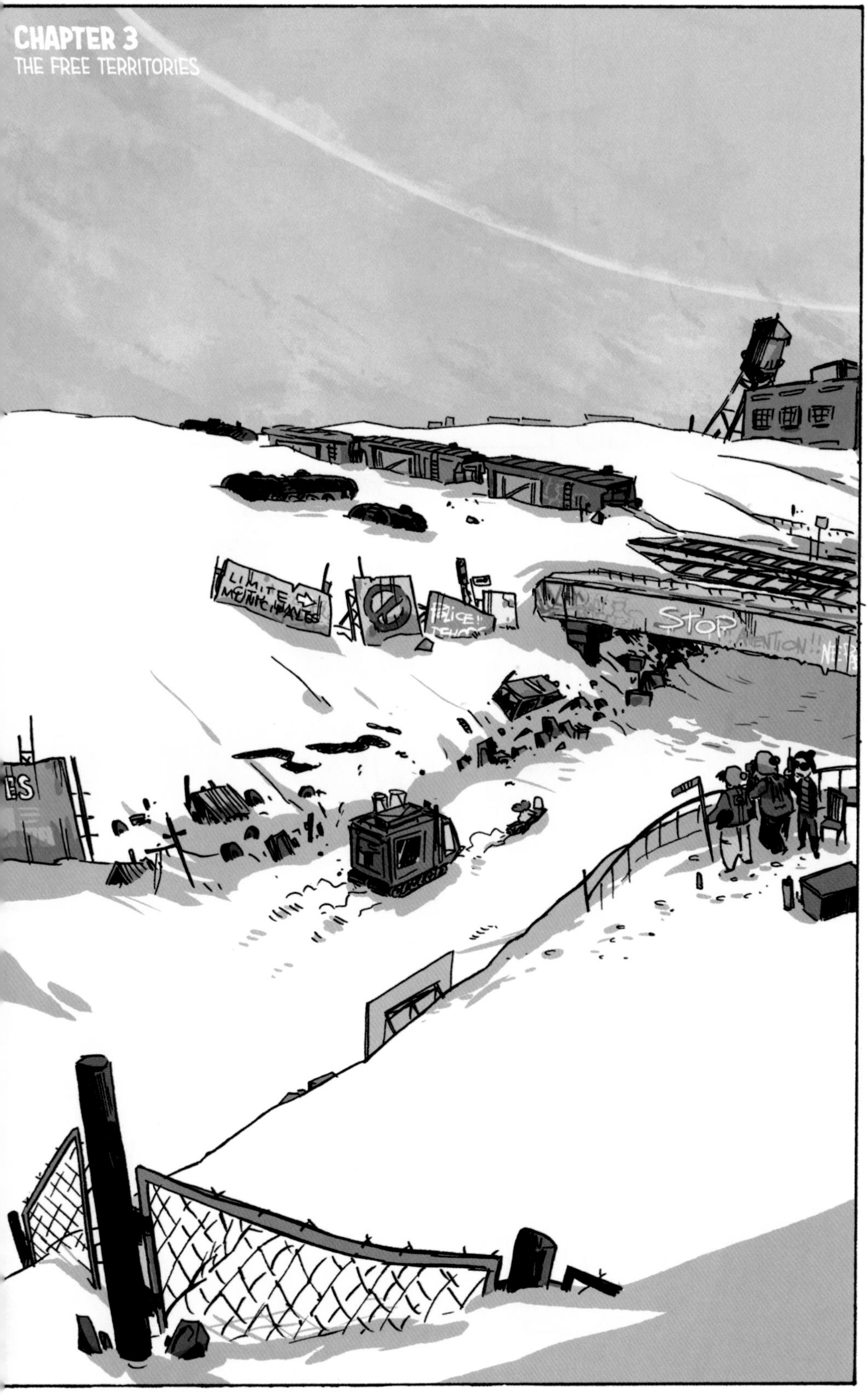
LIMITE MUNICIPALES
STOP

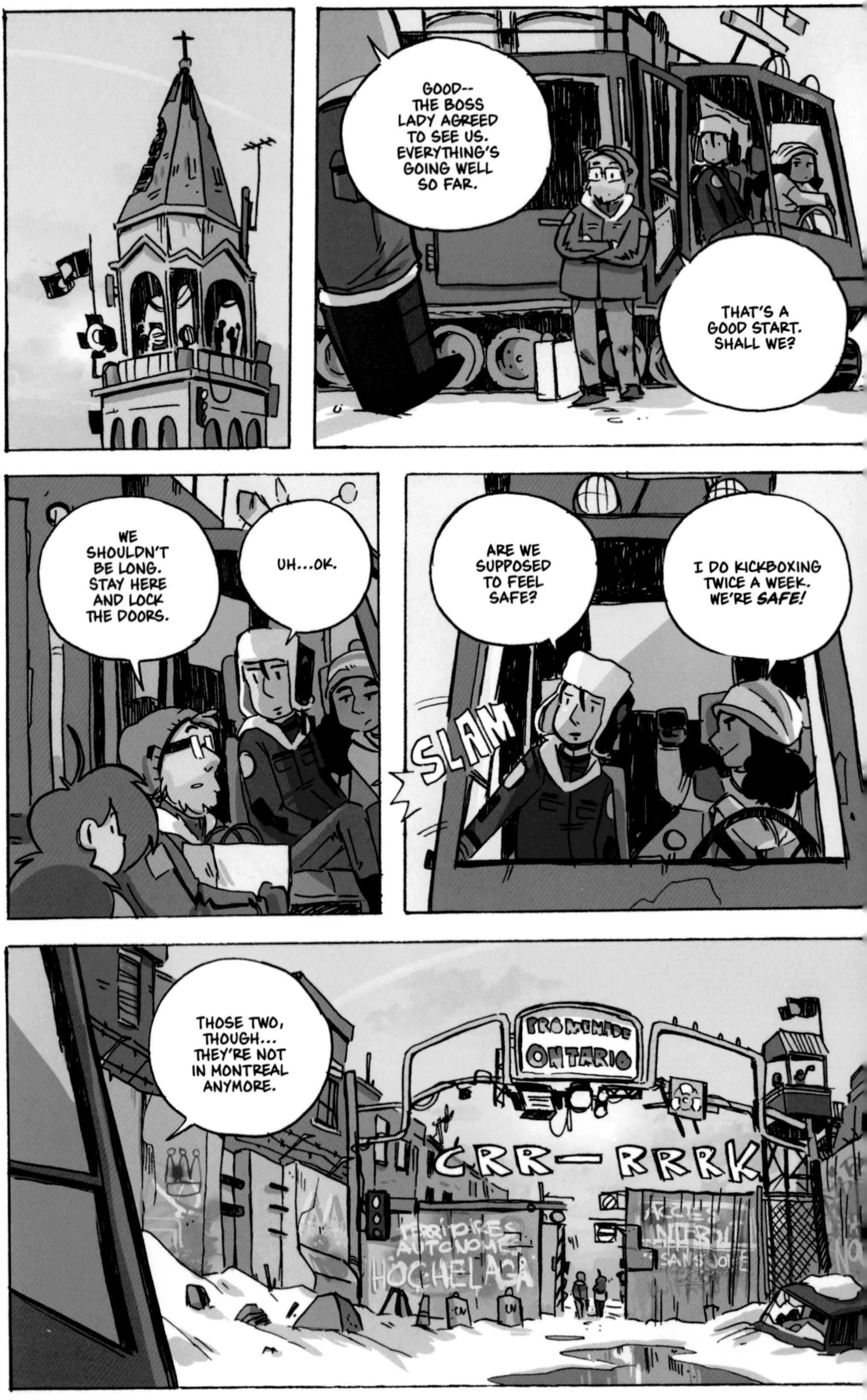
GOOD-- THE BOSS LADY AGREED TO SEE US. EVERYTHING'S GOING WELL SO FAR.
THAT'S A GOOD START. SHALL WE?
WE SHOULDN'T BE LONG. STAY HERE AND LOCK THE DOORS.
UH...OK.
SLAM
ARE WE SUPPOSED TO FEEL SAFE?
I DO KICKBOXING TWICE A WEEK. WE'RE *SAFE!*
THOSE TWO, THOUGH... THEY'RE NOT IN MONTREAL ANYMORE.
PROMENADE
ONTARIO
CRR—RRRK
HOCHELAGA

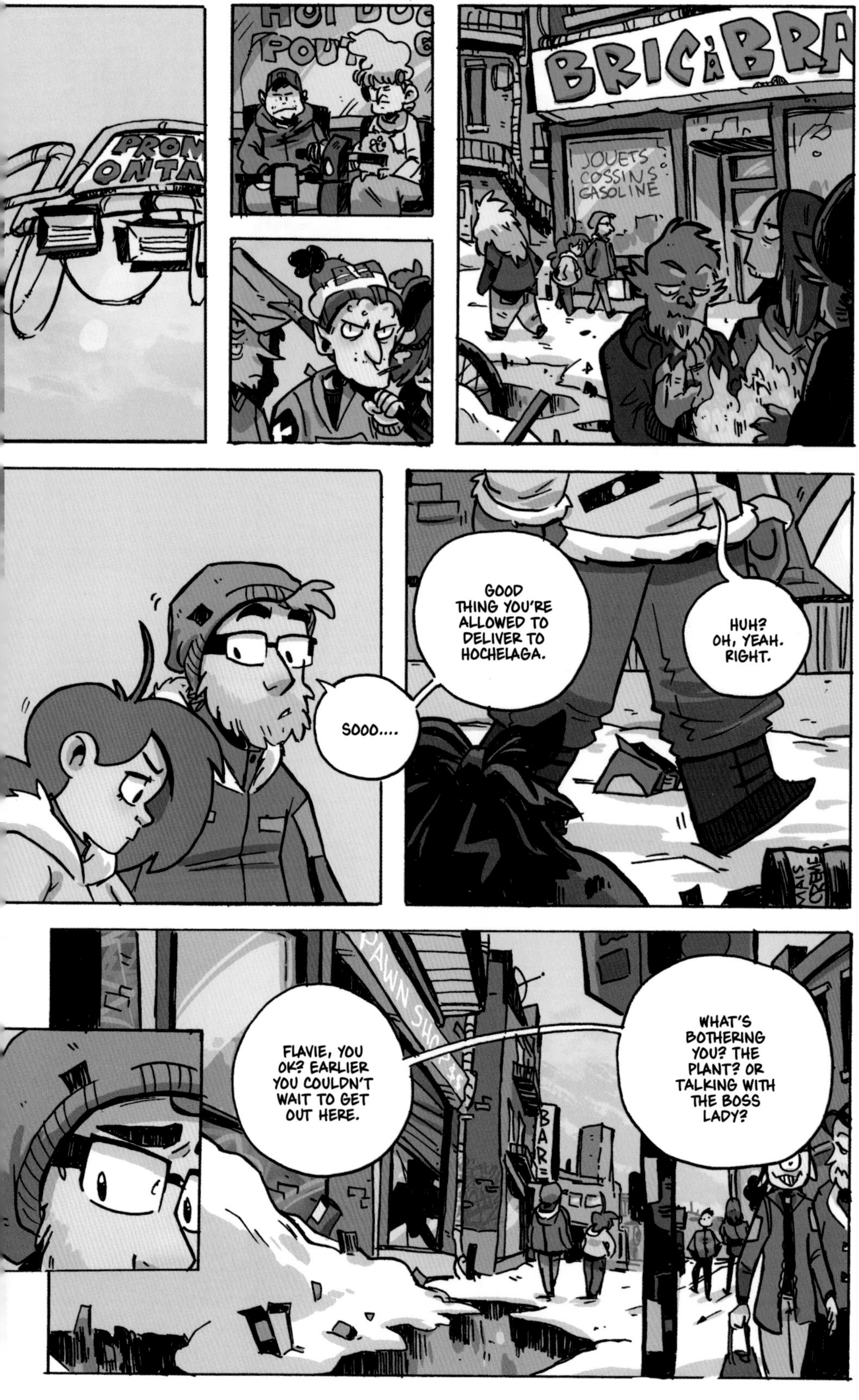
HOT DOG
POUT
PROM
ONTA
BRIC À BRA
JOUETS
COSSINS
GASOLINE
GOOD THING YOU'RE ALLOWED TO DELIVER TO HOCHELAGA.
SOOO....
HUH? OH, YEAH. RIGHT.
MAIS CRÈME
PAWN SHOP
BAR
FLAVIE, YOU OK? EARLIER YOU COULDN'T WAIT TO GET OUT HERE.
WHAT'S BOTHERING YOU? THE PLANT? OR TALKING WITH THE BOSS LADY?

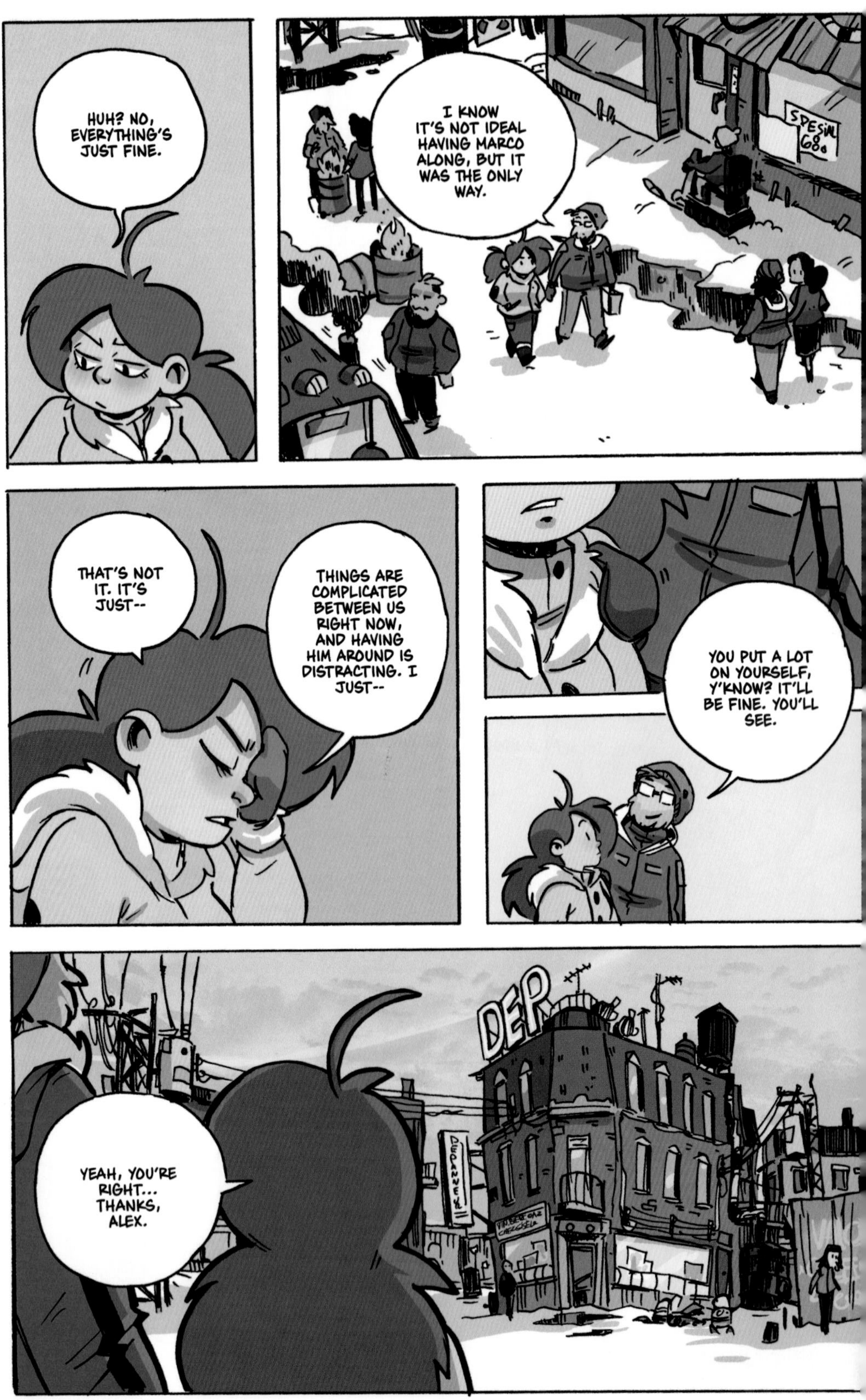
HUH? NO, EVERYTHING'S JUST FINE.
I KNOW IT'S NOT IDEAL HAVING MARCO ALONG, BUT IT WAS THE ONLY WAY.
THAT'S NOT IT. IT'S JUST--
THINGS ARE COMPLICATED BETWEEN US RIGHT NOW, AND HAVING HIM AROUND IS DISTRACTING. I JUST--
YOU PUT A LOT ON YOURSELF, Y'KNOW? IT'LL BE FINE. YOU'LL SEE.
DEP
YEAH, YOU'RE RIGHT... THANKS, ALEX.

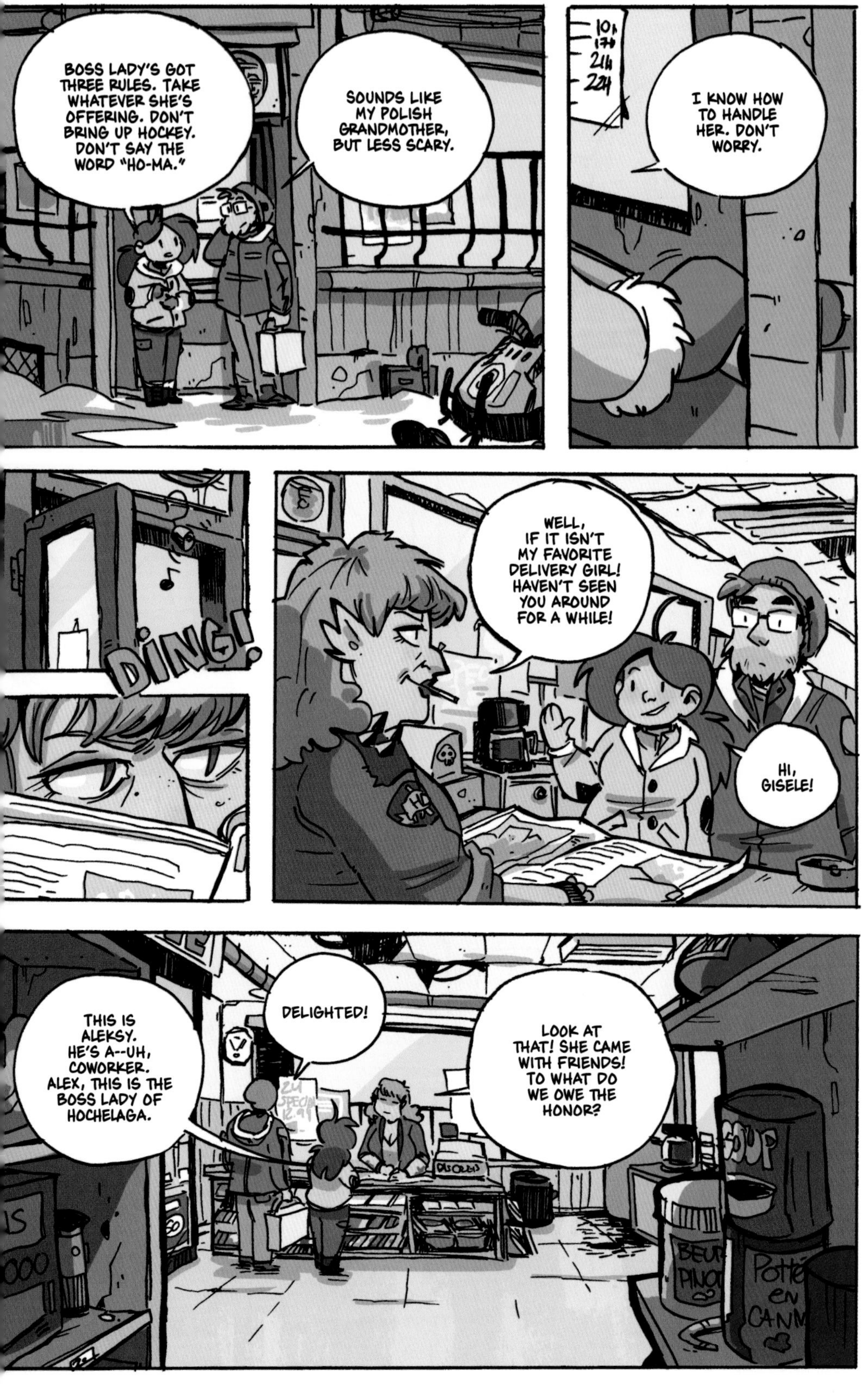
BOSS LADY'S GOT THREE RULES. TAKE WHATEVER SHE'S OFFERING. DON'T BRING UP HOCKEY. DON'T SAY THE WORD "HO-MA."
SOUNDS LIKE MY POLISH GRANDMOTHER, BUT LESS SCARY.
I KNOW HOW TO HANDLE HER. DON'T WORRY.
DING!
WELL, IF IT ISN'T MY FAVORITE DELIVERY GIRL! HAVEN'T SEEN YOU AROUND FOR A WHILE!
HI, GISELE!
THIS IS ALEKSY. HE'S A--UH, COWORKER. ALEX, THIS IS THE BOSS LADY OF HOCHELAGA.
DELIGHTED!
LOOK AT THAT! SHE CAME WITH FRIENDS! TO WHAT DO WE OWE THE HONOR?
SOUP

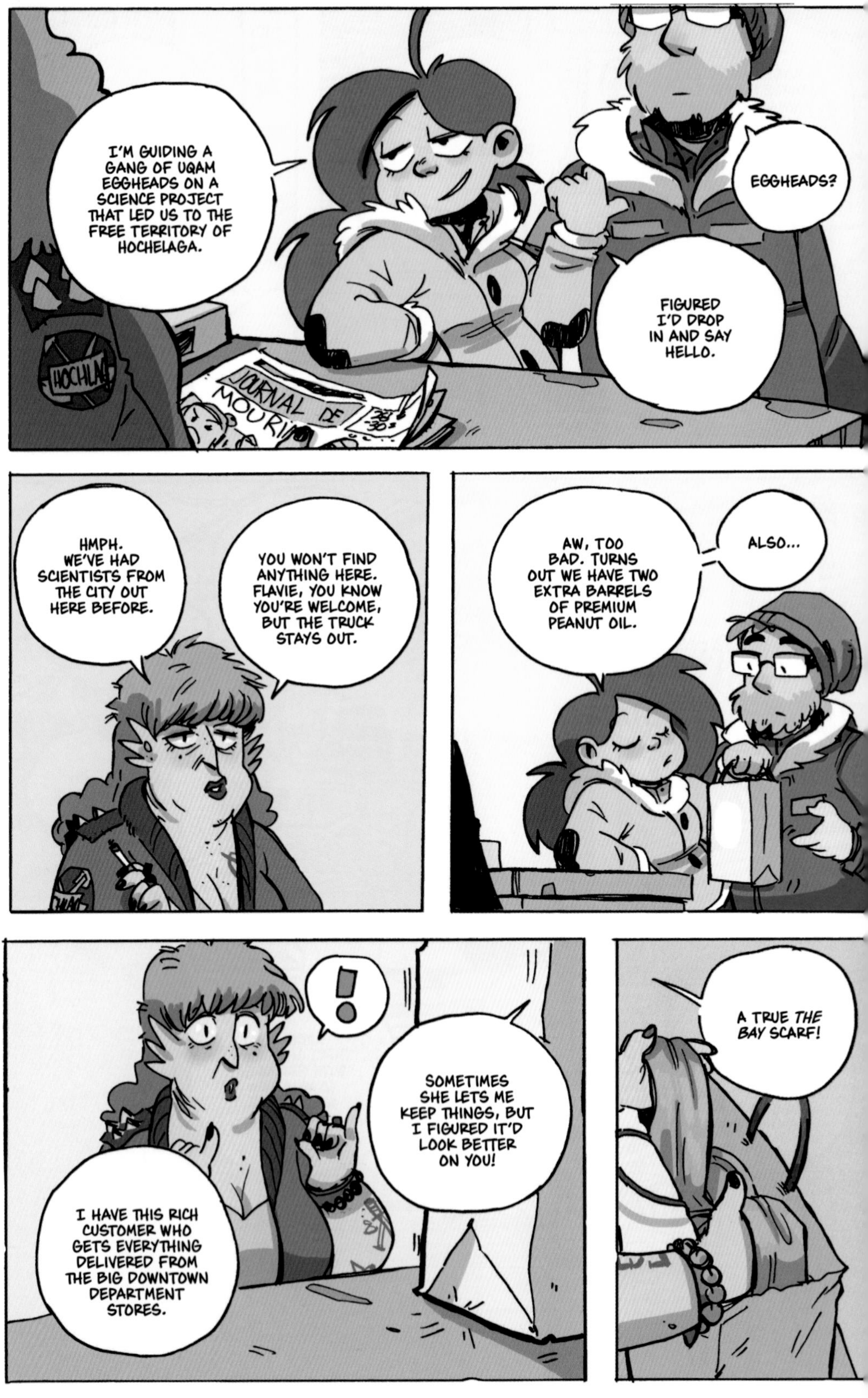
I'M GUIDING A GANG OF UQAM EGGHEADS ON A SCIENCE PROJECT THAT LED US TO THE FREE TERRITORY OF HOCHELAGA.
EGGHEADS?
FIGURED I'D DROP IN AND SAY HELLO.
JOURNAL DE MOURI
HOCHLAG
HMPH. WE'VE HAD SCIENTISTS FROM THE CITY OUT HERE BEFORE.
YOU WON'T FIND ANYTHING HERE. FLAVIE, YOU KNOW YOU'RE WELCOME, BUT THE TRUCK STAYS OUT.
AW, TOO BAD. TURNS OUT WE HAVE TWO EXTRA BARRELS OF PREMIUM PEANUT OIL.
ALSO...
!
I HAVE THIS RICH CUSTOMER WHO GETS EVERYTHING DELIVERED FROM THE BIG DOWNTOWN DEPARTMENT STORES.
SOMETIMES SHE LETS ME KEEP THINGS, BUT I FIGURED IT'D LOOK BETTER ON YOU!
A TRUE *THE BAY* SCARF!

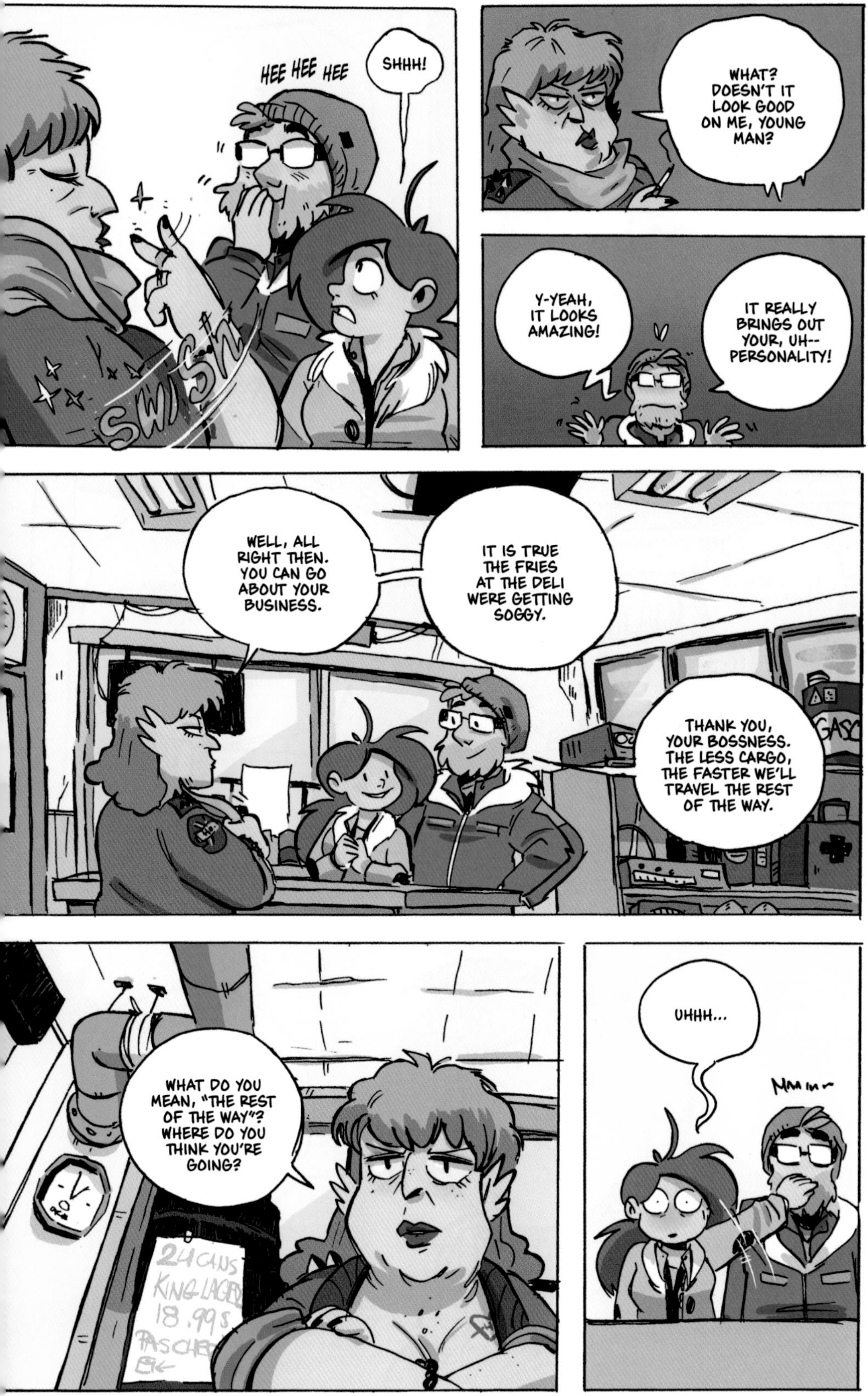
HEE HEE HEE
SHHH!
WHAT? DOESN'T IT LOOK GOOD ON ME, YOUNG MAN?
Y-YEAH, IT LOOKS AMAZING!
IT REALLY BRINGS OUT YOUR, UH-- PERSONALITY!
WELL, ALL RIGHT THEN. YOU CAN GO ABOUT YOUR BUSINESS.
IT IS TRUE THE FRIES AT THE DELI WERE GETTING SOGGY.
THANK YOU, YOUR BOSSNESS. THE LESS CARGO, THE FASTER WE'LL TRAVEL THE REST OF THE WAY.
WHAT DO YOU MEAN, "THE REST OF THE WAY"? WHERE DO YOU THINK YOU'RE GOING?
24 CANS
UHHH...

IT'S JUST...I HAVE TO TAKE THEM EAST, PAST VIAU. IF YOU COULD LET US THROUGH THE NEIGHBORHOOD--

WHAT NEXT? A PONY?

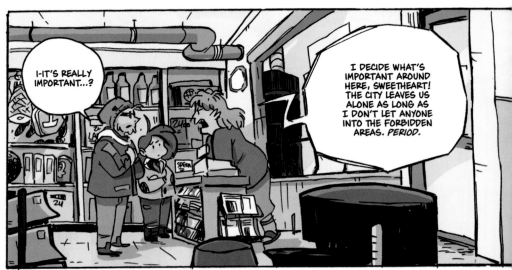

I-IT'S REALLY IMPORTANT...?

I DECIDE WHAT'S IMPORTANT AROUND HERE, SWEETHEART! THE CITY LEAVES US ALONE AS LONG AS I DON'T LET ANYONE INTO THE FORBIDDEN AREAS. *PERIOD.*

C'MON, GISELE. WE HAVE NO CHOICE. IF WE CAN'T CROSS THROUGH HOCHELAGA, THE OTHER ROUTES ARE SUICIDE. PLEASE.

YOU'RE TAKING THIS PRETTY PERSONALLY FOR A MERE GUIDE.

I WAS GRANDSTANDING EARLIER. THIS IS VERY PERSONAL.

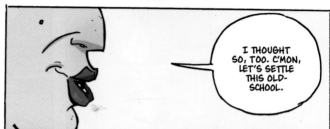

I THOUGHT SO, TOO. C'MON, LET'S SETTLE THIS OLD-SCHOOL.

WITH A GOOD OL' FASHIONED ARM WRESTLE!

BAM!

YOU WON YOUR RIGHT TO COME HERE THE DAY YOU BEAT ME, REMEMBER? WELL, I WANT A REMATCH.

IT'S BEEN A WHILE. I... CAN'T.

OH, COME ON!

AHEM. EXCUSE US A MOMENT.

C'MON, FLAVIE! I SAW YOU LIFT A HUNDRED-POUND ANTENNA WITH ONE HAND!

YOU'RE EXAGGERATING.

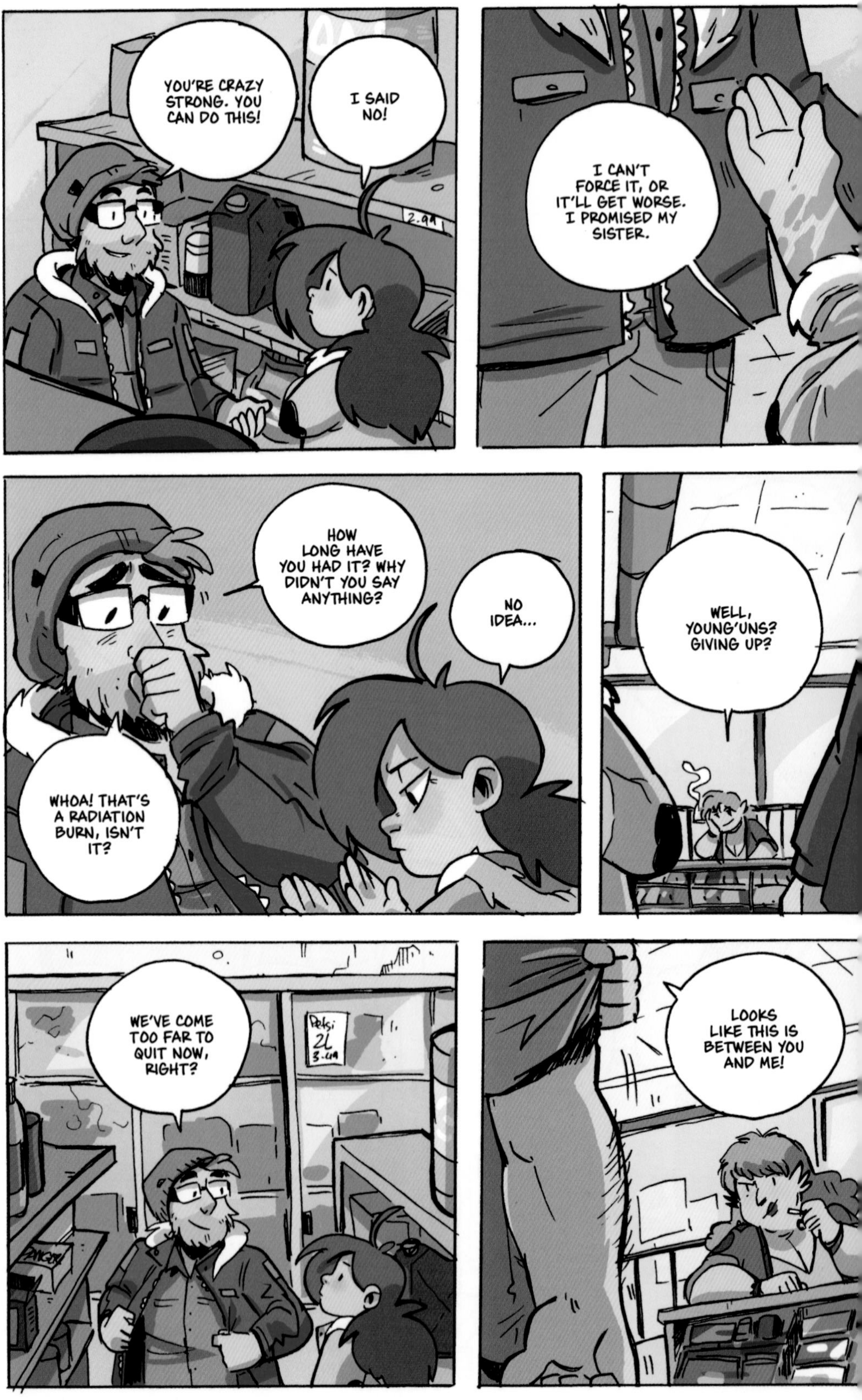
YOU'RE CRAZY STRONG. YOU CAN DO THIS!
I SAID NO!
I CAN'T FORCE IT, OR IT'LL GET WORSE. I PROMISED MY SISTER.
HOW LONG HAVE YOU HAD IT? WHY DIDN'T YOU SAY ANYTHING?
NO IDEA...
WHOA! THAT'S A RADIATION BURN, ISN'T IT?
WELL, YOUNG'UNS? GIVING UP?
WE'VE COME TOO FAR TO QUIT NOW, RIGHT?
LOOKS LIKE THIS IS BETWEEN YOU AND ME!

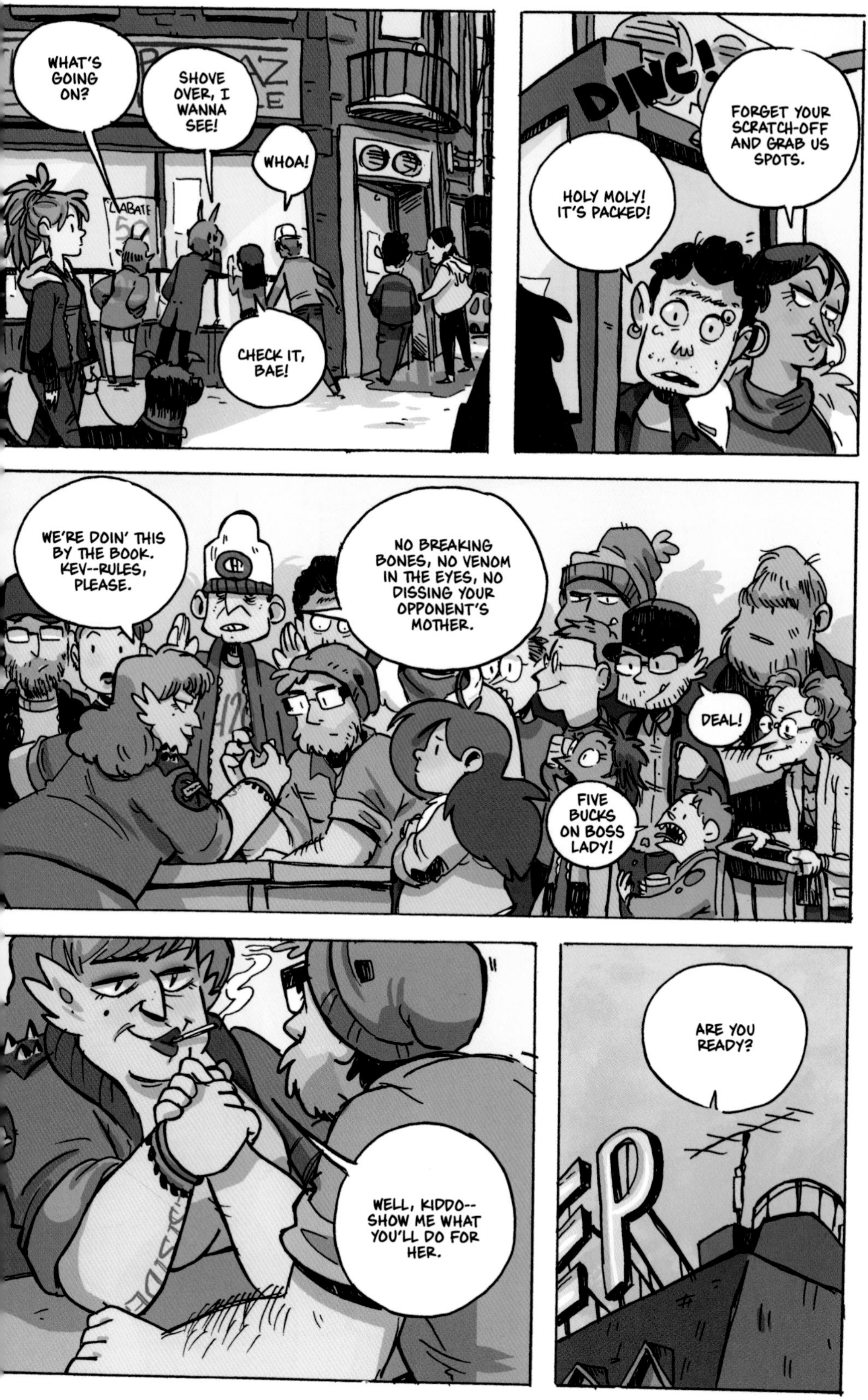
WHAT'S GOING ON?
SHOVE OVER, I WANNA SEE!
WHOA!
CHECK IT, BAE!
DING!
FORGET YOUR SCRATCH-OFF AND GRAB US SPOTS.
HOLY MOLY! IT'S PACKED!
WE'RE DOIN' THIS BY THE BOOK. KEV--RULES, PLEASE.
NO BREAKING BONES, NO VENOM IN THE EYES, NO DISSING YOUR OPPONENT'S MOTHER.
DEAL!
FIVE BUCKS ON BOSS LADY!
WELL, KIDDO-- SHOW ME WHAT YOU'LL DO FOR HER.
ARE YOU READY?

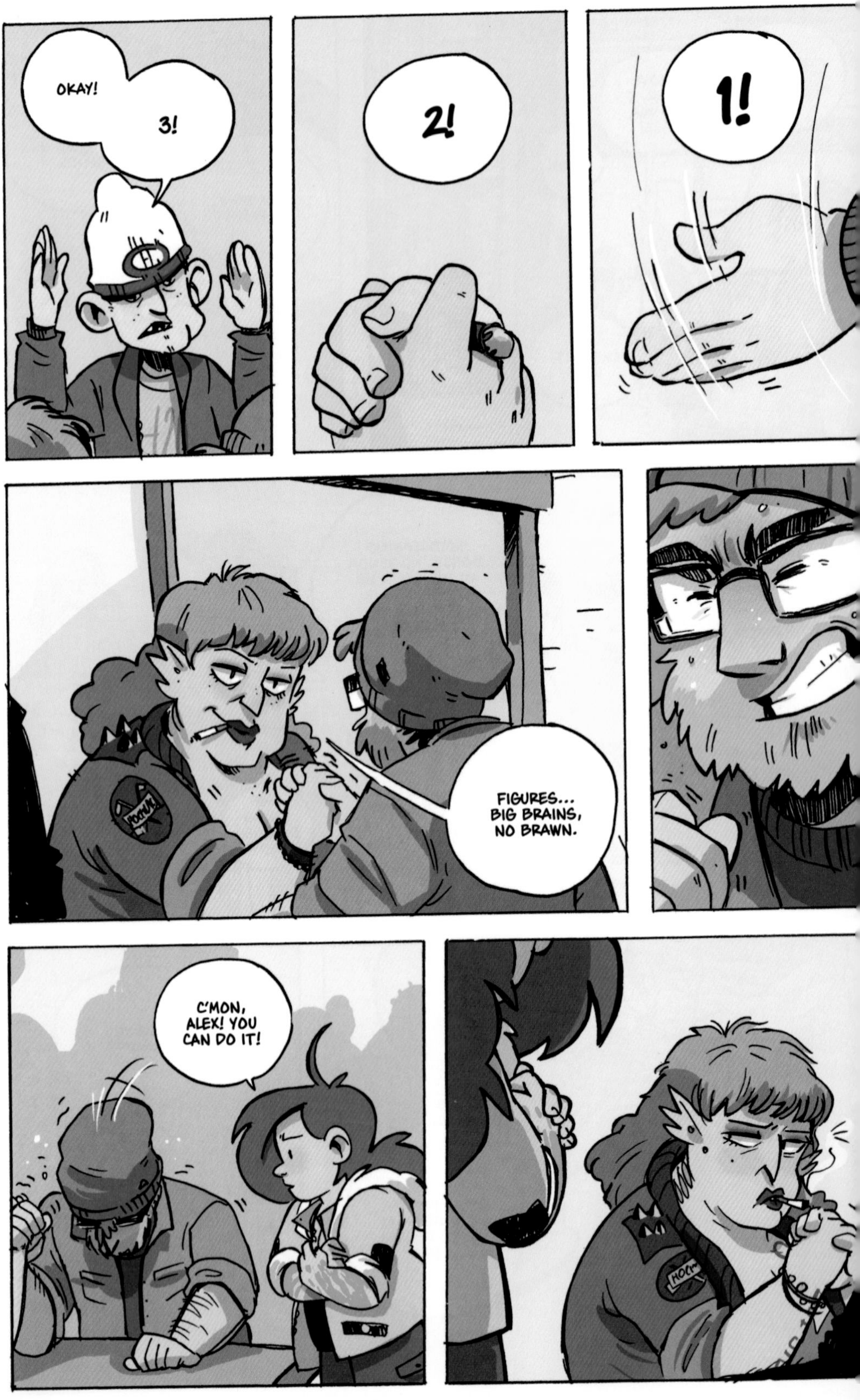
OKAY!
3!
2!
1!
FIGURES... BIG BRAINS, NO BRAWN.
C'MON, ALEX! YOU CAN DO IT!

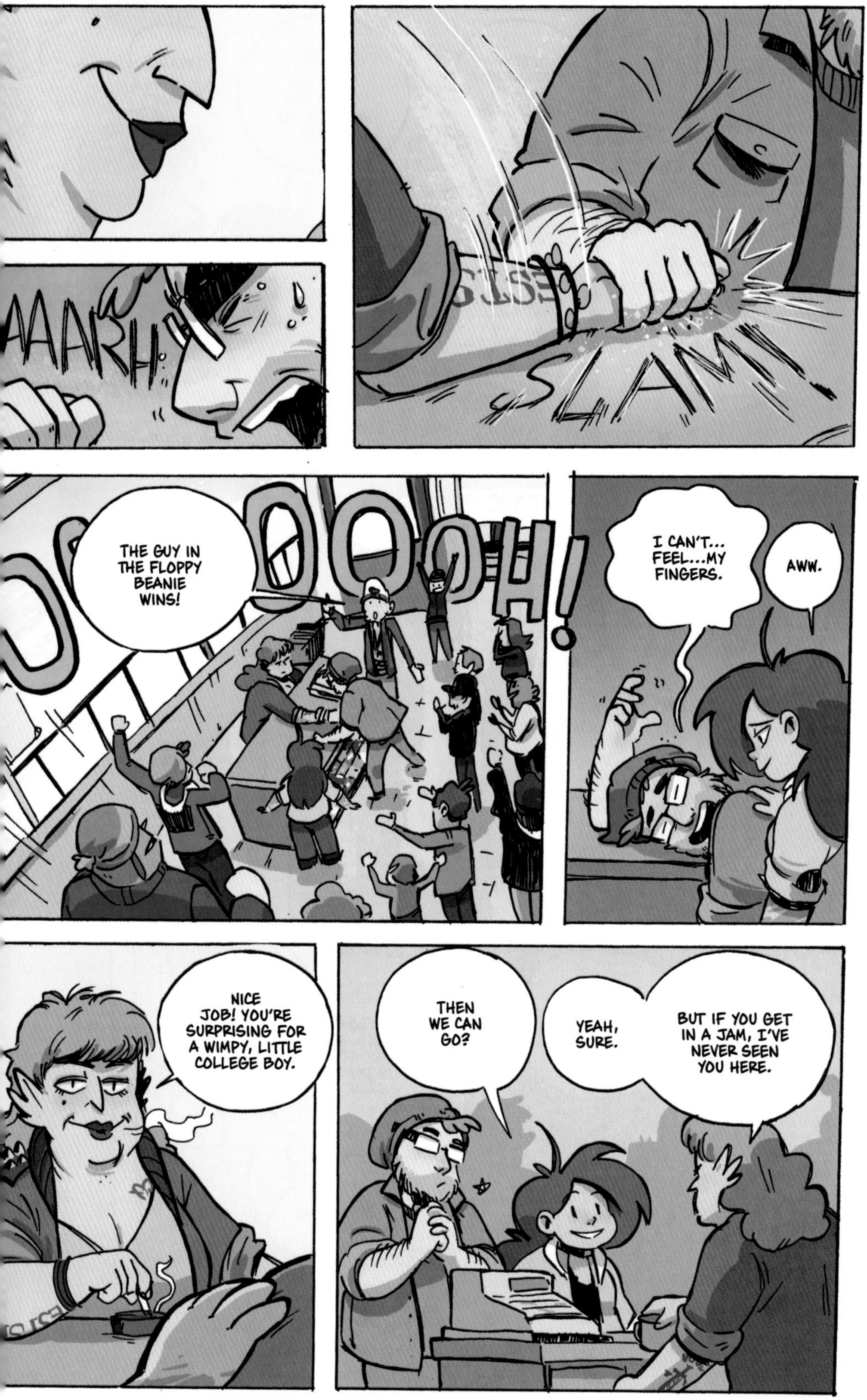
AAARH
SLAM!
THE GUY IN THE FLOPPY BEANIE WINS!
OOOOH!
I CAN'T... FEEL...MY FINGERS.
AWW.
NICE JOB! YOU'RE SURPRISING FOR A WIMPY, LITTLE COLLEGE BOY.
THEN WE CAN GO?
YEAH, SURE.
BUT IF YOU GET IN A JAM, I'VE NEVER SEEN YOU HERE.

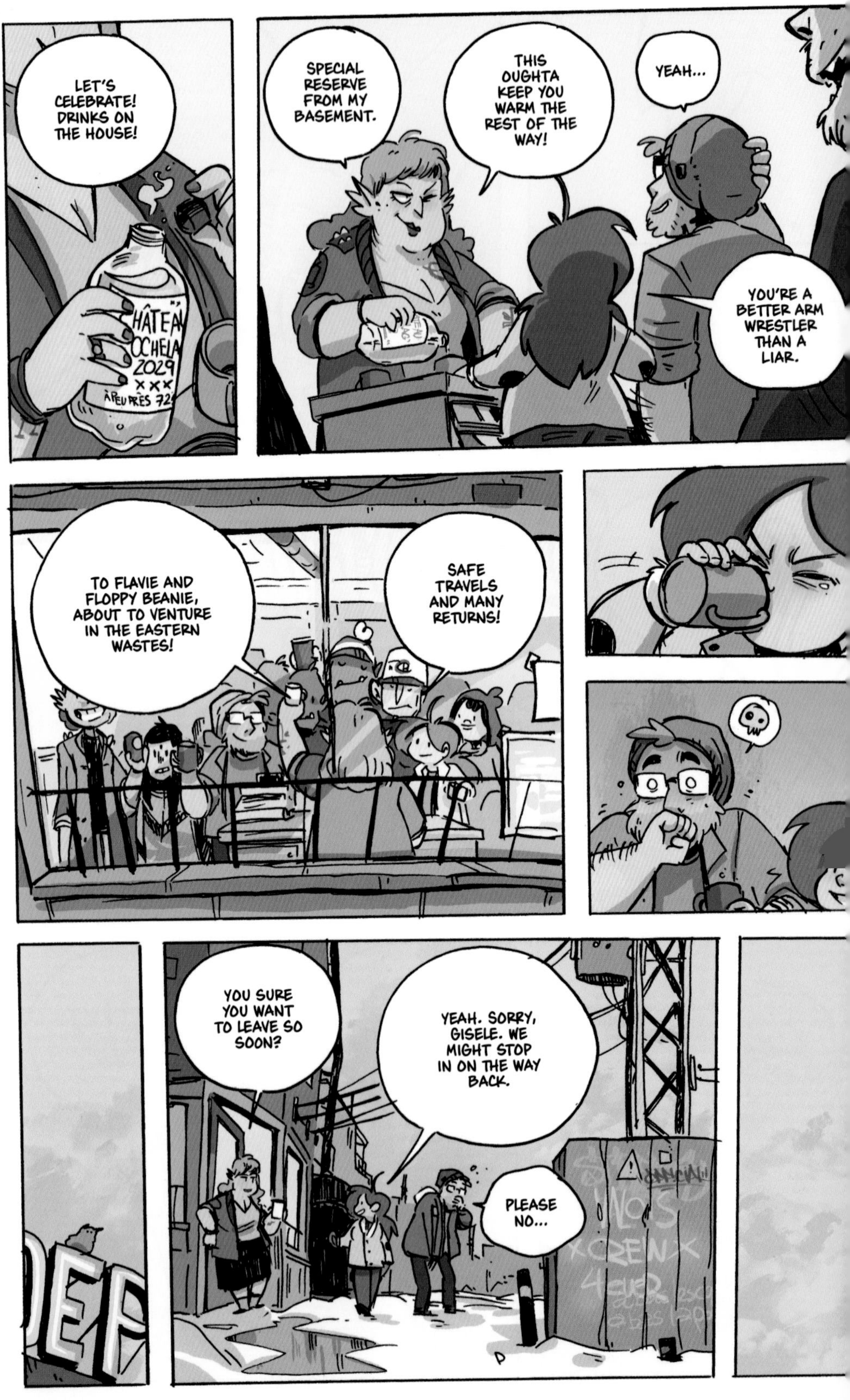
LET'S CELEBRATE! DRINKS ON THE HOUSE!
CHÂTEAU COCHELAG 2029 XXX À PEU PRÈS 72
SPECIAL RESERVE FROM MY BASEMENT.
THIS OUGHTA KEEP YOU WARM THE REST OF THE WAY!
YEAH...
YOU'RE A BETTER ARM WRESTLER THAN A LIAR.
TO FLAVIE AND FLOPPY BEANIE, ABOUT TO VENTURE IN THE EASTERN WASTES!
SAFE TRAVELS AND MANY RETURNS!
YOU SURE YOU WANT TO LEAVE SO SOON?
YEAH. SORRY, GISELE. WE MIGHT STOP IN ON THE WAY BACK.
PLEASE NO...

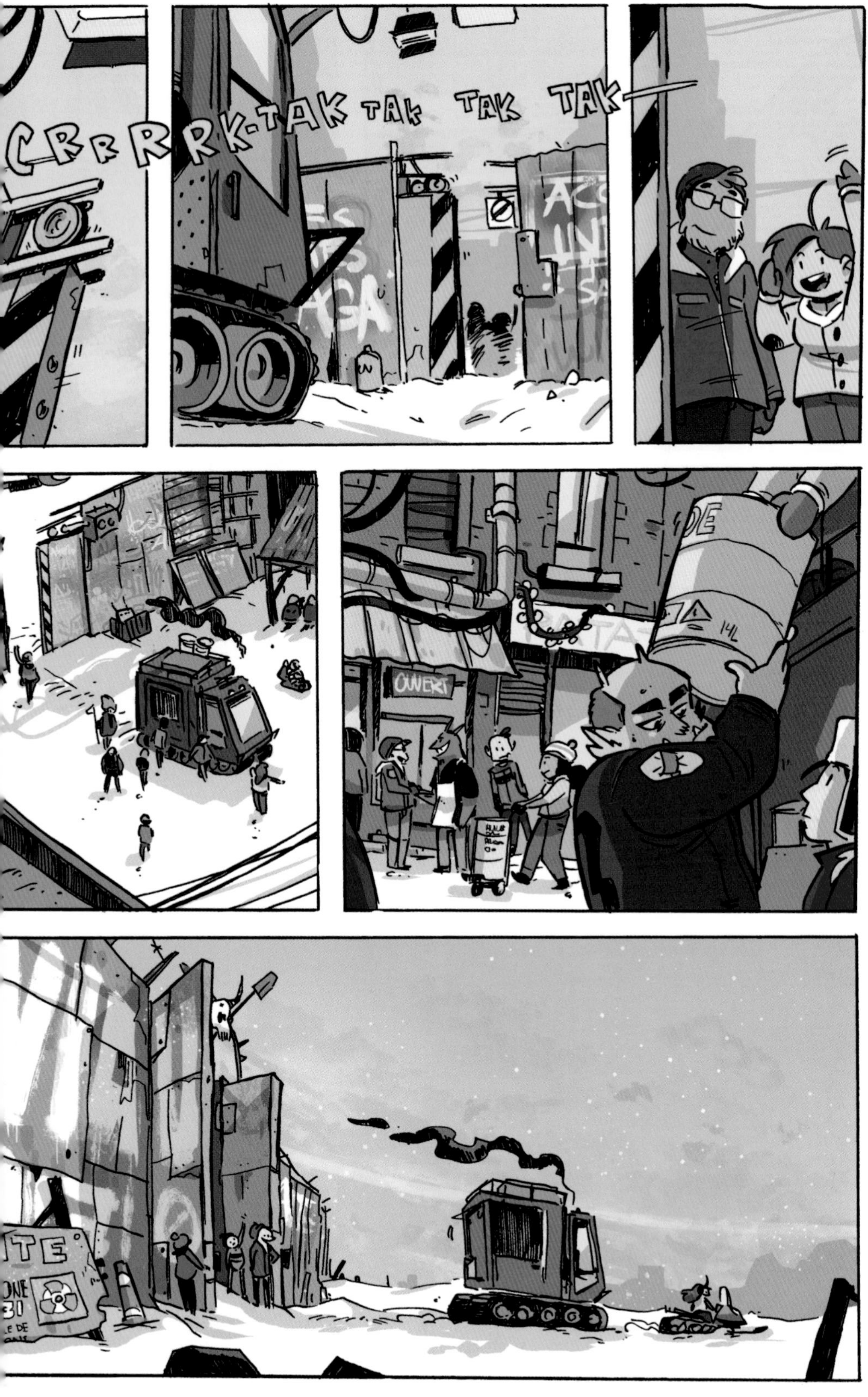
CRRRRK-TAK TAK TAK TAK—
OUVERT
14L

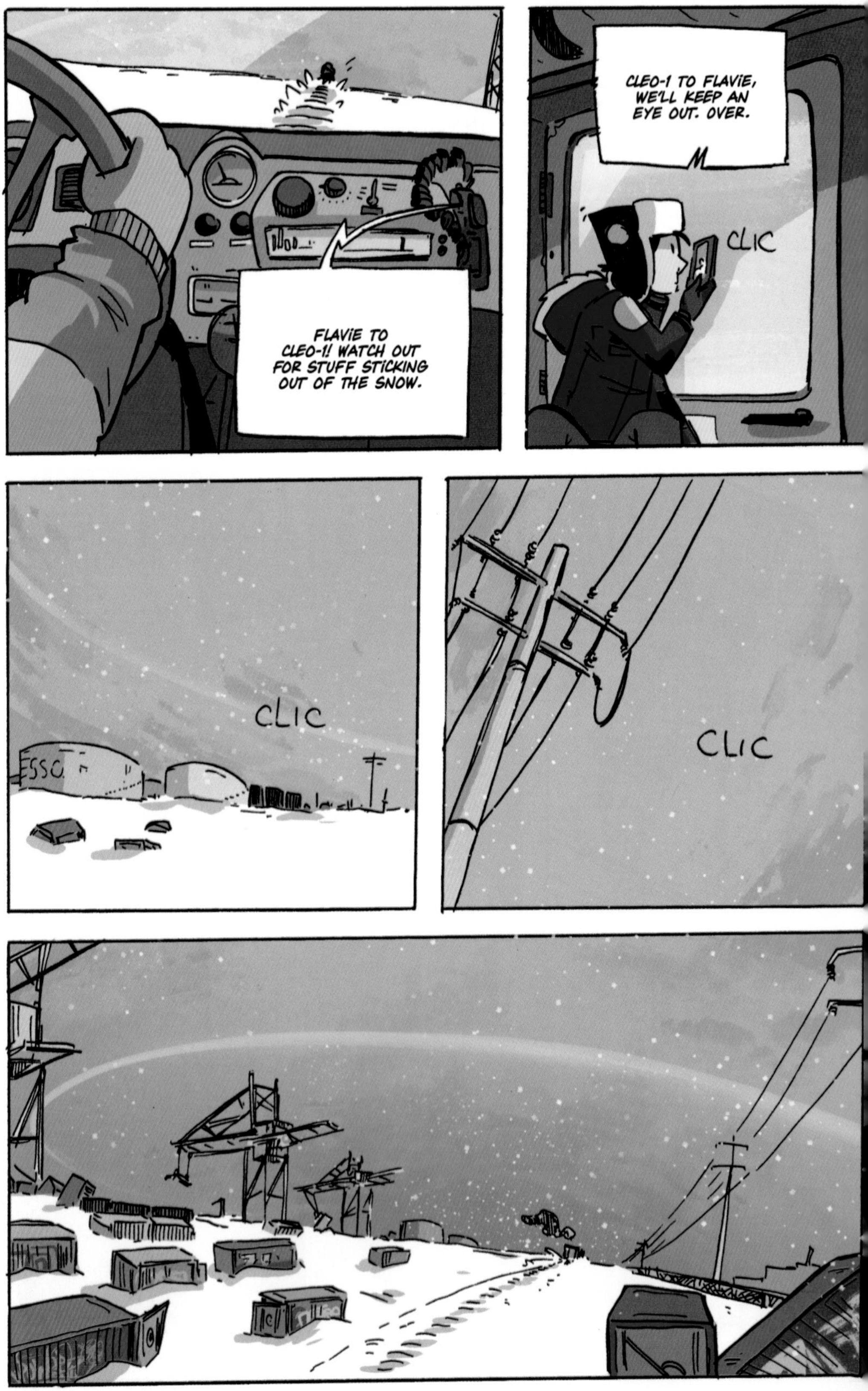

FLAVIE TO CLEO-1! WATCH OUT FOR STUFF STICKING OUT OF THE SNOW.
CLEO-1 TO FLAVIE, WE'LL KEEP AN EYE OUT. OVER.
CLIC
ESSO
CLIC
CLIC

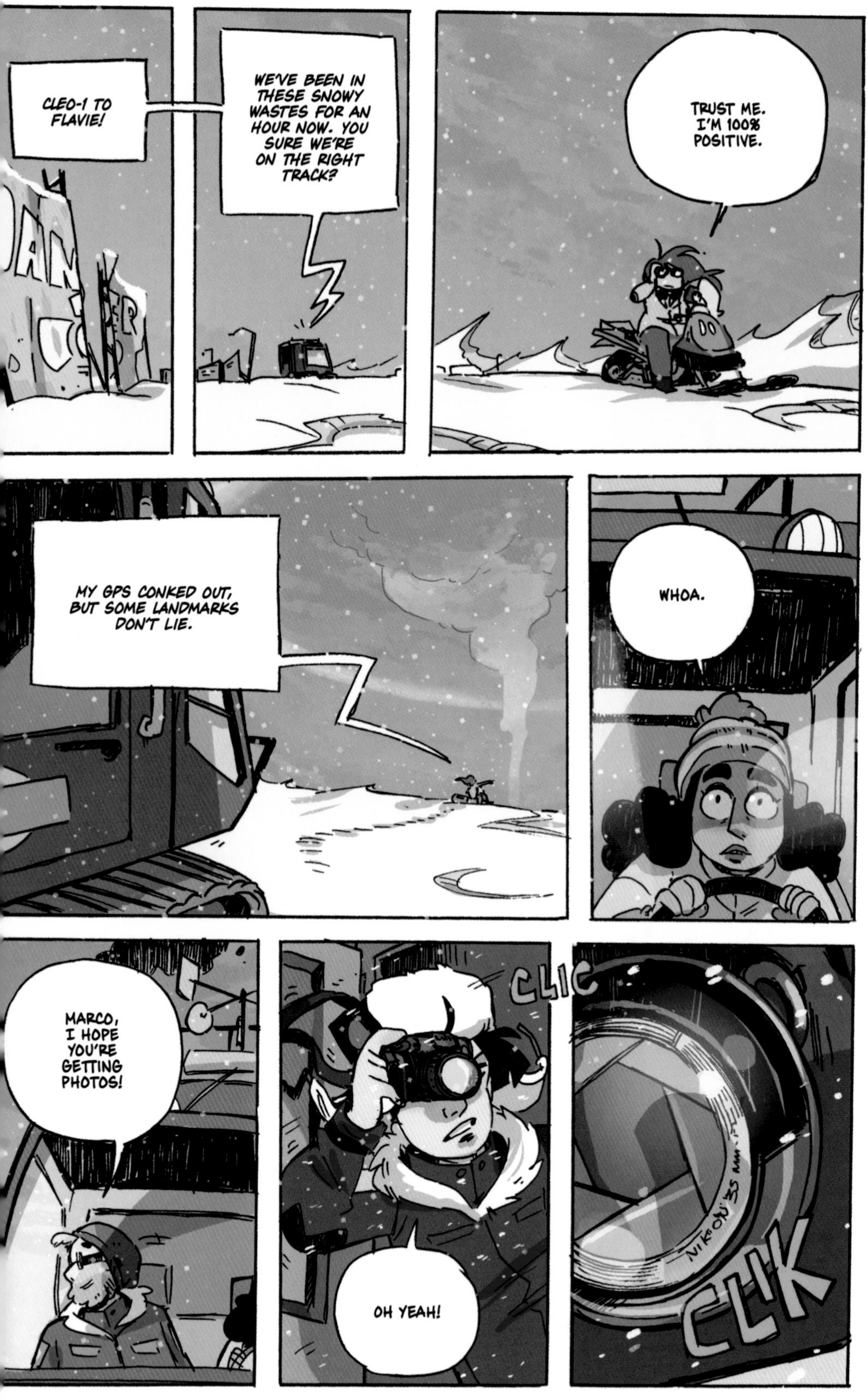
CLEO-1 TO FLAVIE!
WE'VE BEEN IN THESE SNOWY WASTES FOR AN HOUR NOW. YOU SURE WE'RE ON THE RIGHT TRACK?
TRUST ME. I'M 100% POSITIVE.
MY GPS CONKED OUT, BUT SOME LANDMARKS DON'T LIE.
WHOA.
MARCO, I HOPE YOU'RE GETTING PHOTOS!
CLIC
OH YEAH!
CLIK

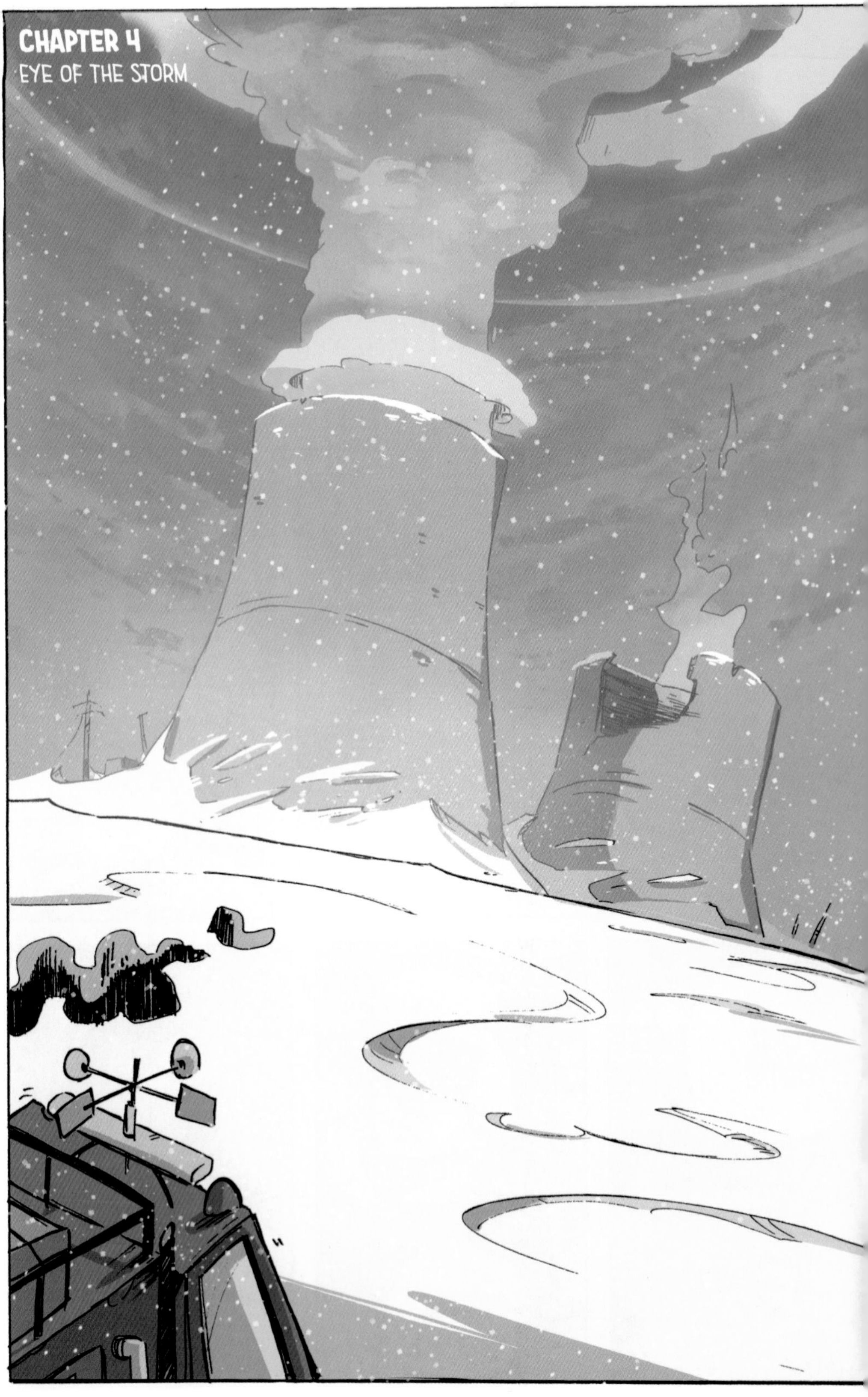
CHAPTER 4
EYE OF THE STORM

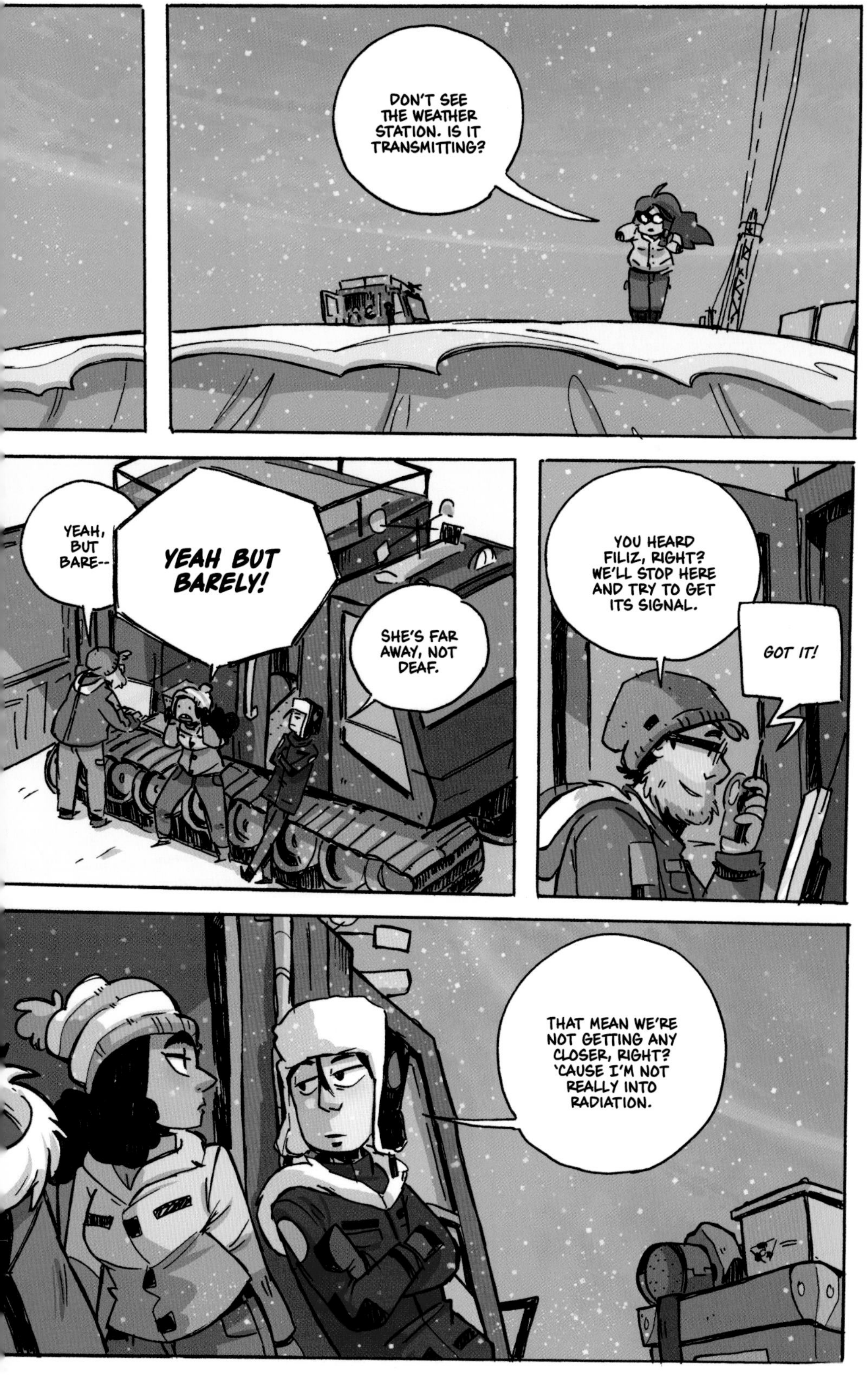
DON'T SEE THE WEATHER STATION. IS IT TRANSMITTING?
YEAH, BUT BARE--
YEAH BUT BARELY!
SHE'S FAR AWAY, NOT DEAF.
YOU HEARD FILIZ, RIGHT? WE'LL STOP HERE AND TRY TO GET ITS SIGNAL.
GOT IT!
THAT MEAN WE'RE NOT GETTING ANY CLOSER, RIGHT? 'CAUSE I'M NOT REALLY INTO RADIATION.

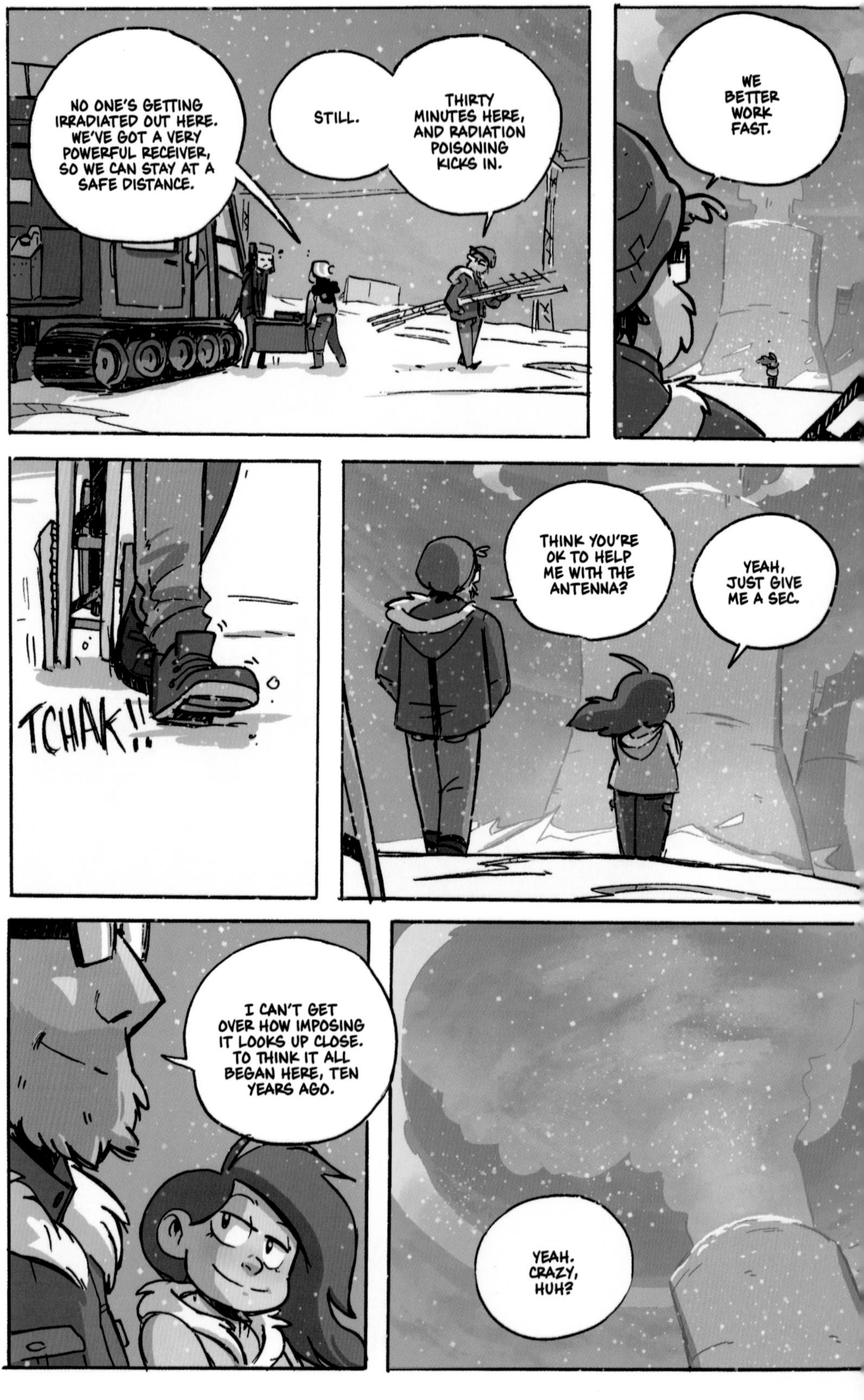
NO ONE'S GETTING IRRADIATED OUT HERE. WE'VE GOT A VERY POWERFUL RECEIVER, SO WE CAN STAY AT A SAFE DISTANCE.
STILL.
THIRTY MINUTES HERE, AND RADIATION POISONING KICKS IN.
WE BETTER WORK FAST.
TCHAK!!
THINK YOU'RE OK TO HELP ME WITH THE ANTENNA?
YEAH, JUST GIVE ME A SEC.
I CAN'T GET OVER HOW IMPOSING IT LOOKS UP CLOSE. TO THINK IT ALL BEGAN HERE, TEN YEARS AGO.
YEAH. CRAZY, HUH?

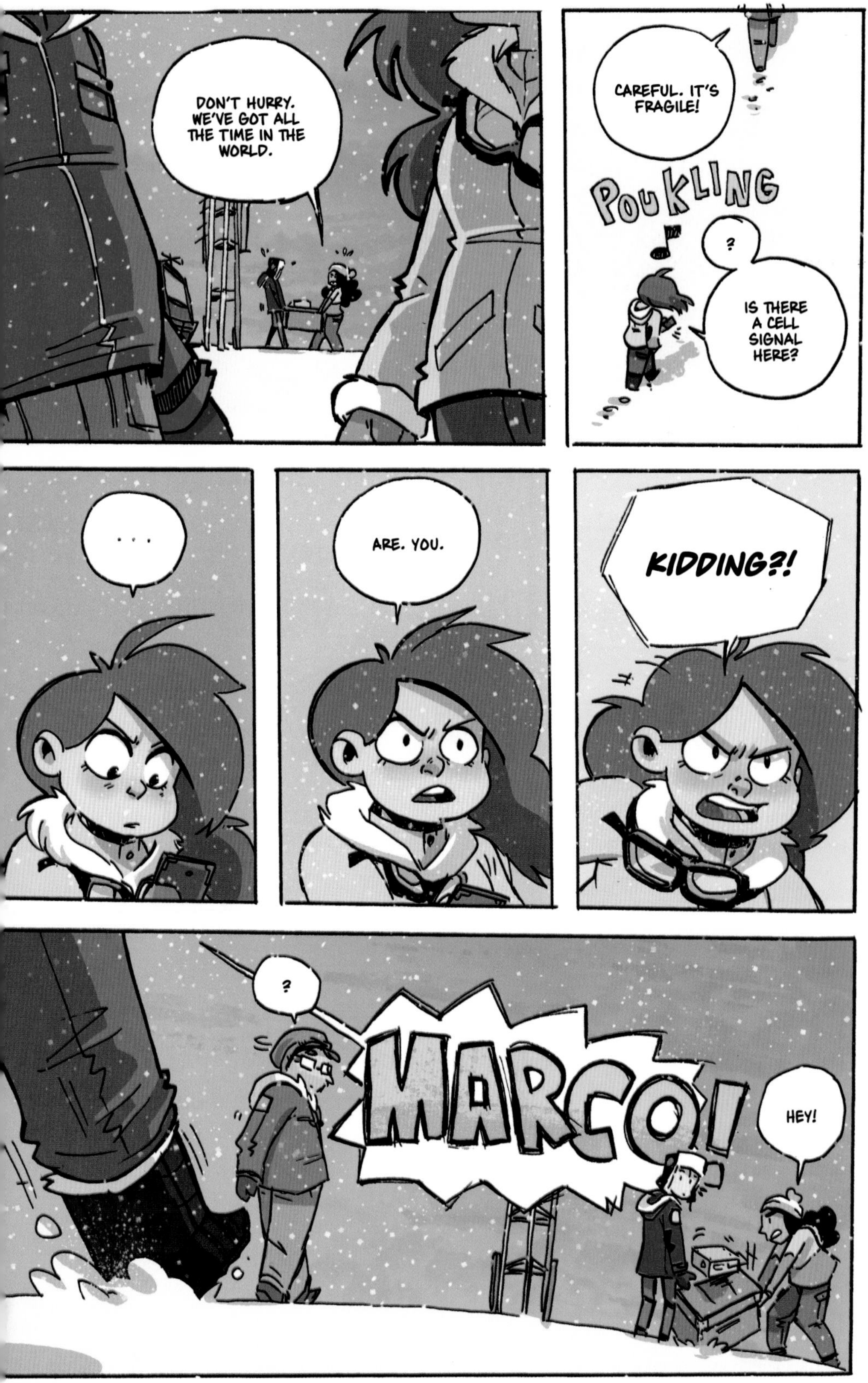
DON'T HURRY. WE'VE GOT ALL THE TIME IN THE WORLD.
CAREFUL. IT'S FRAGILE!
POUKLING
?
IS THERE A CELL SIGNAL HERE?
. . .
ARE. YOU.
KIDDING?!
?
MARCO!
HEY!

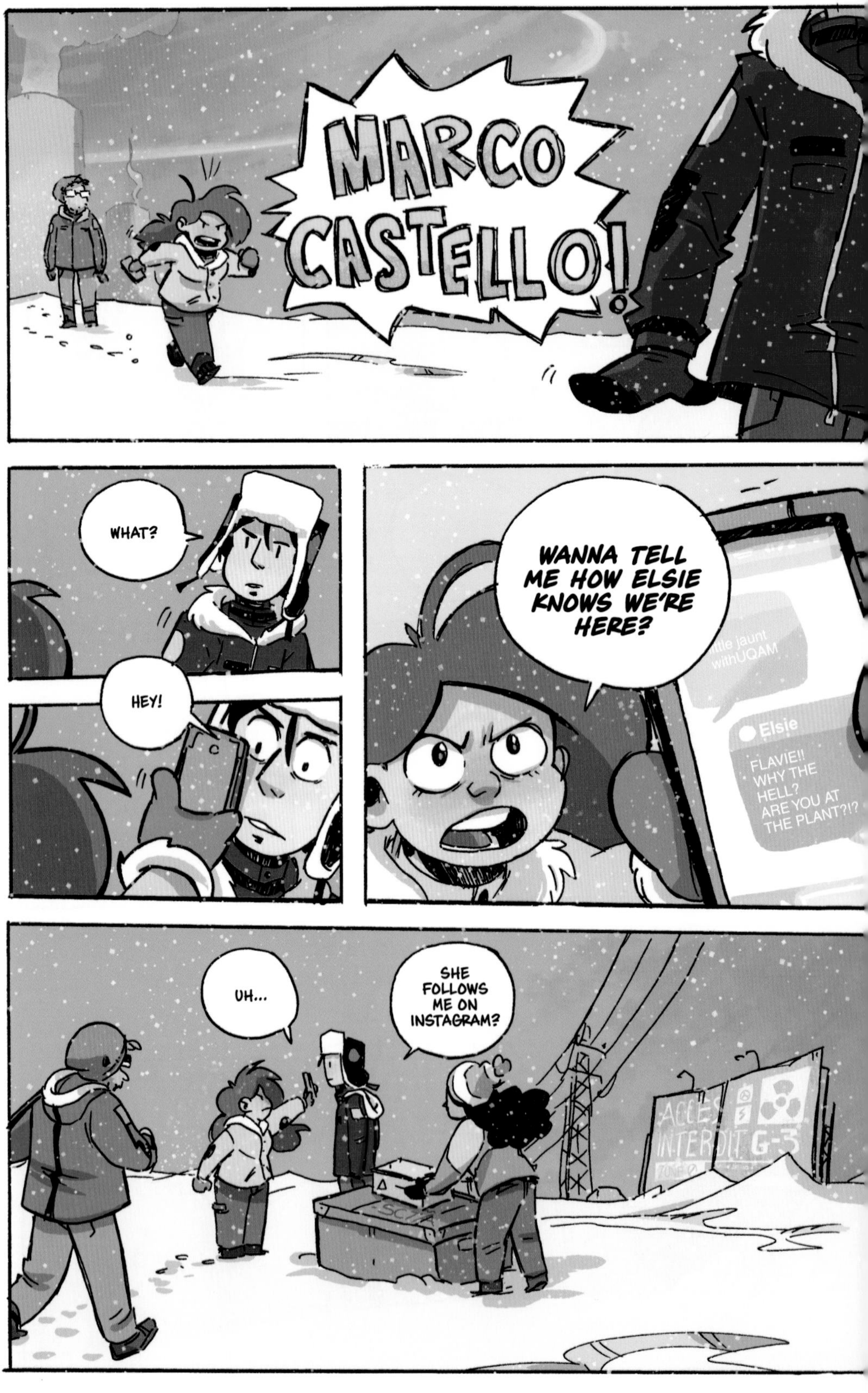
MARCO CASTELLO!
WHAT?
HEY!
WANNA TELL ME HOW ELSIE KNOWS WE'RE HERE?
Elsie
FLAVIE!! WHY THE HELL? ARE YOU AT THE PLANT?!?
UH...
SHE FOLLOWS ME ON INSTAGRAM?
ACCES INTERDIT G-3

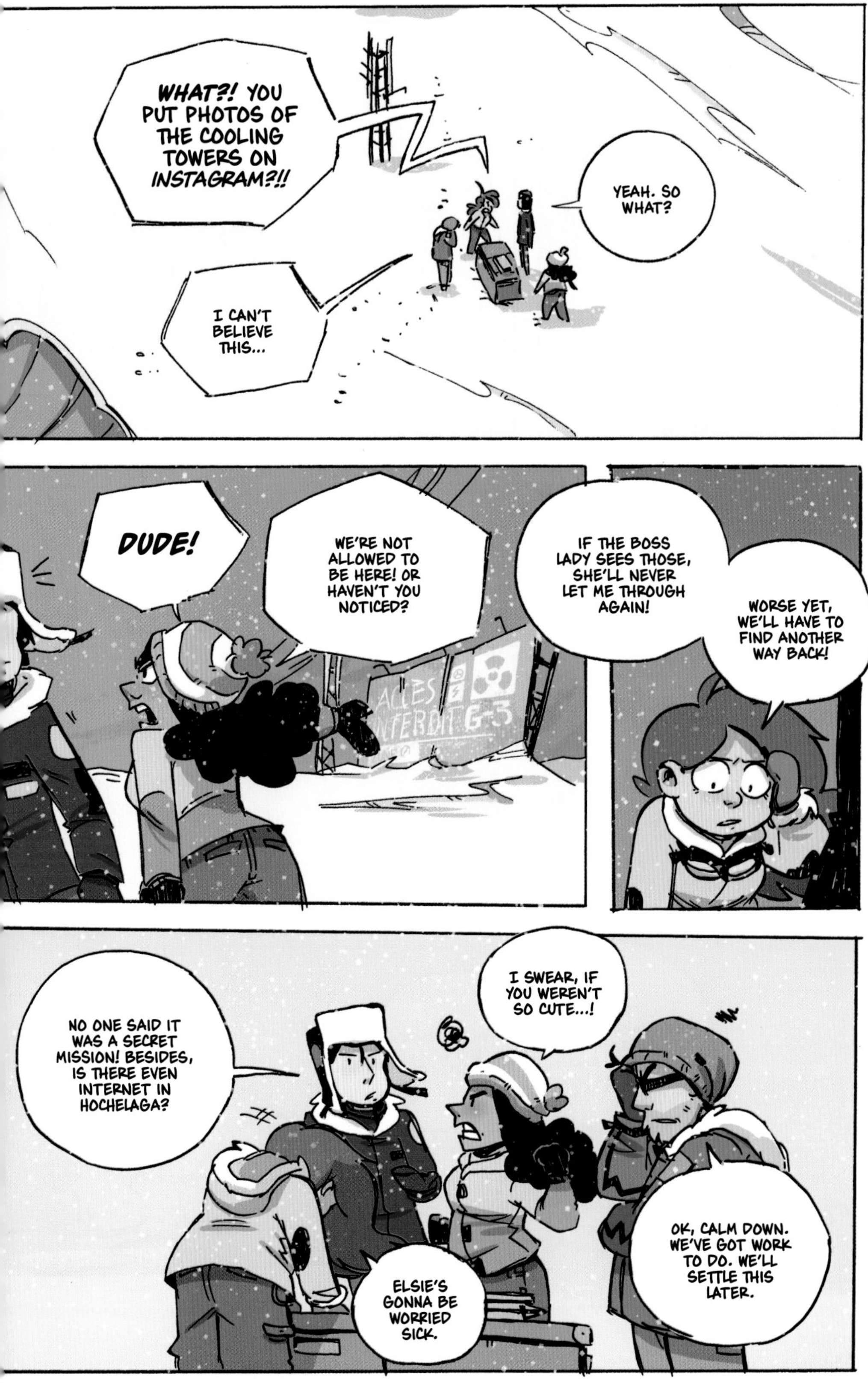
WHAT?! YOU PUT PHOTOS OF THE COOLING TOWERS ON INSTAGRAM?!!
YEAH. SO WHAT?
I CAN'T BELIEVE THIS...
DUDE!
WE'RE NOT ALLOWED TO BE HERE! OR HAVEN'T YOU NOTICED?
IF THE BOSS LADY SEES THOSE, SHE'LL NEVER LET ME THROUGH AGAIN!
WORSE YET, WE'LL HAVE TO FIND ANOTHER WAY BACK!
NO ONE SAID IT WAS A SECRET MISSION! BESIDES, IS THERE EVEN INTERNET IN HOCHELAGA?
I SWEAR, IF YOU WEREN'T SO CUTE...!
ELSIE'S GONNA BE WORRIED SICK.
OK, CALM DOWN. WE'VE GOT WORK TO DO. WE'LL SETTLE THIS LATER.

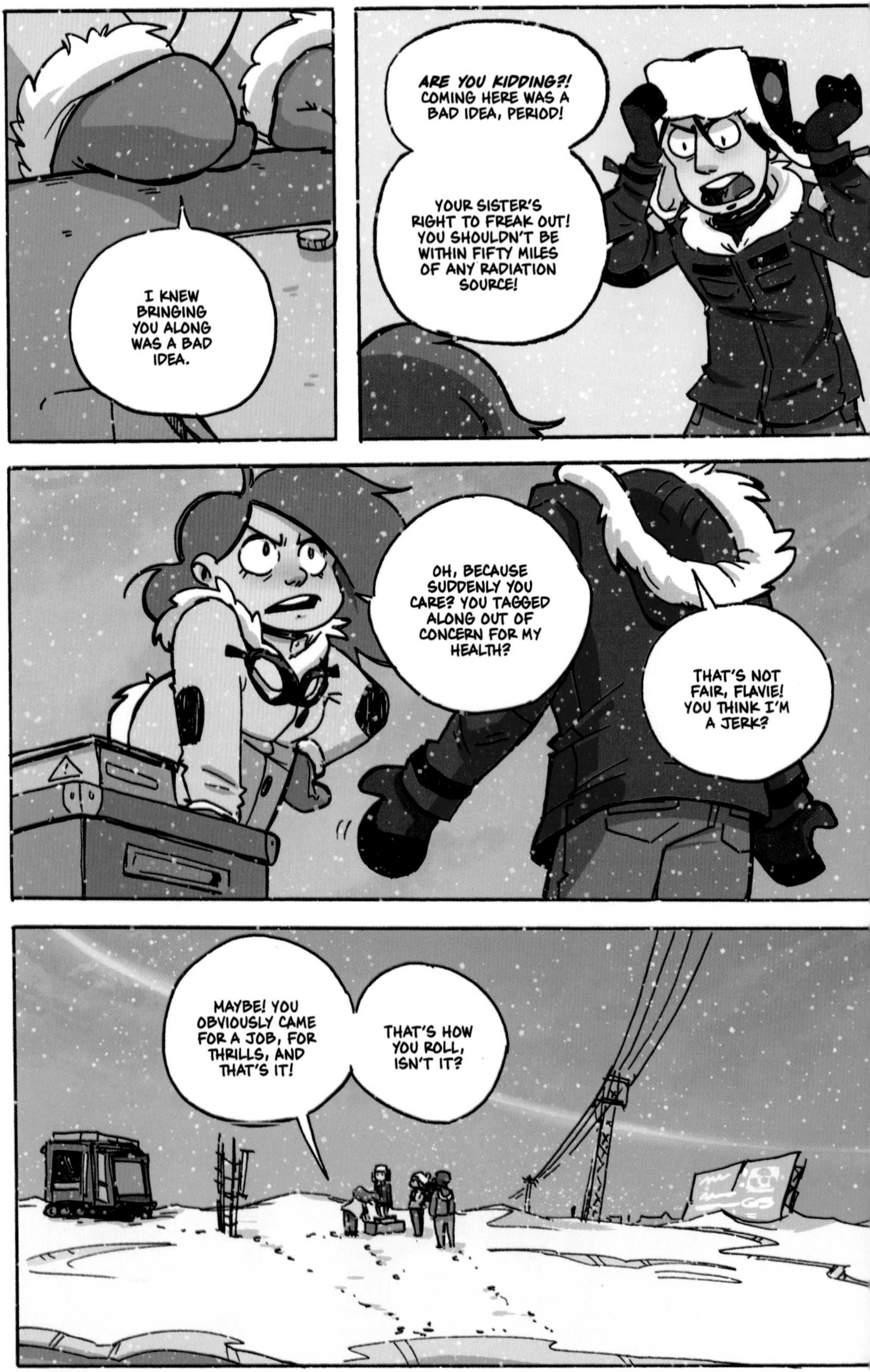
I KNEW BRINGING YOU ALONG WAS A BAD IDEA.
ARE YOU KIDDING?! COMING HERE WAS A BAD IDEA, PERIOD!
YOUR SISTER'S RIGHT TO FREAK OUT! YOU SHOULDN'T BE WITHIN FIFTY MILES OF ANY RADIATION SOURCE!
OH, BECAUSE SUDDENLY YOU CARE? YOU TAGGED ALONG OUT OF CONCERN FOR MY HEALTH?
THAT'S NOT FAIR, FLAVIE! YOU THINK I'M A JERK?
MAYBE! YOU OBVIOUSLY CAME FOR A JOB, FOR THRILLS, AND THAT'S IT!
THAT'S HOW YOU ROLL, ISN'T IT?

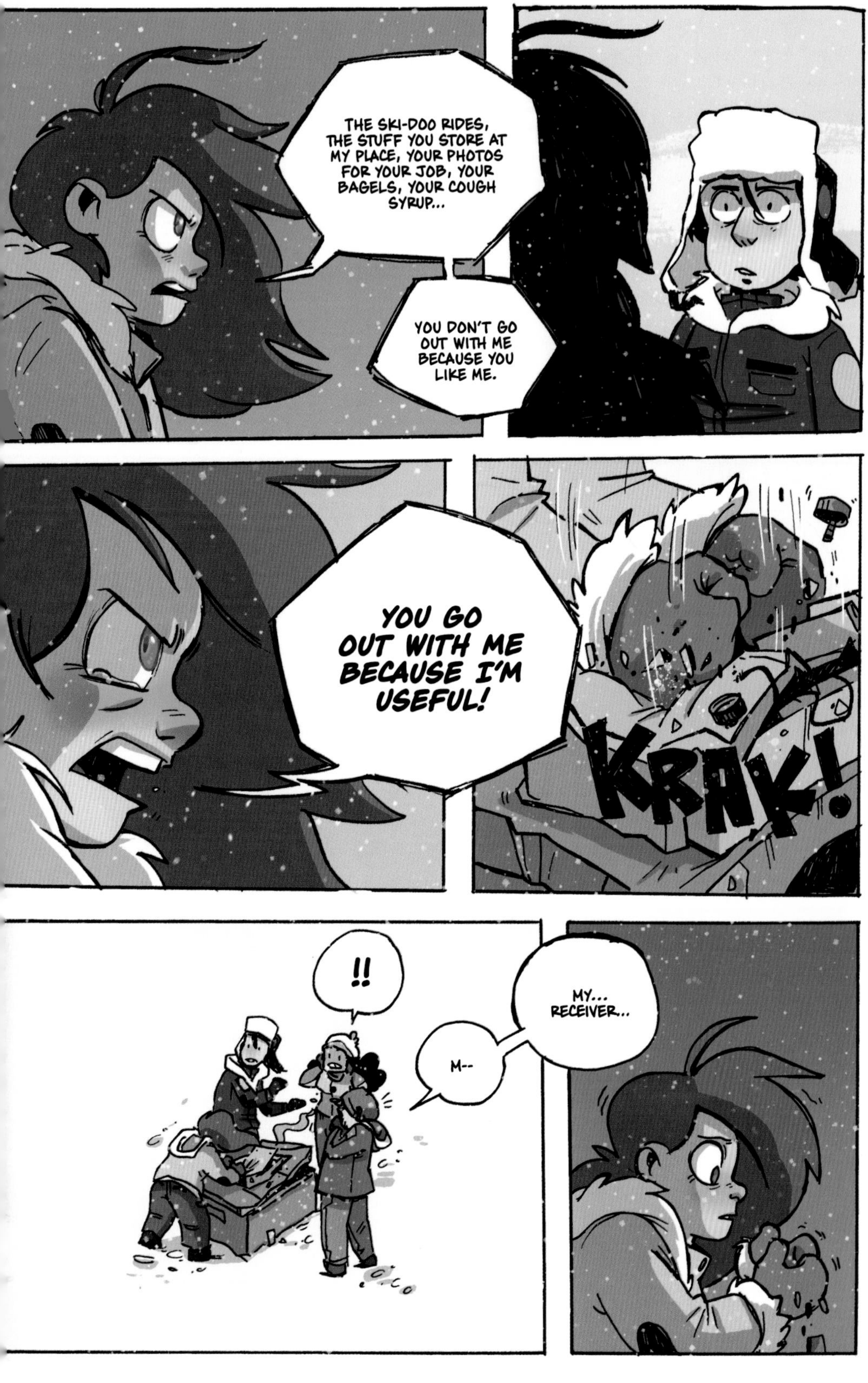
THE SKI-DOO RIDES, THE STUFF YOU STORE AT MY PLACE, YOUR PHOTOS FOR YOUR JOB, YOUR BAGELS, YOUR COUGH SYRUP...
YOU DON'T GO OUT WITH ME BECAUSE YOU LIKE ME.
YOU GO OUT WITH ME BECAUSE I'M USEFUL!
KRAK!
!!
M--
MY... RECEIVER...

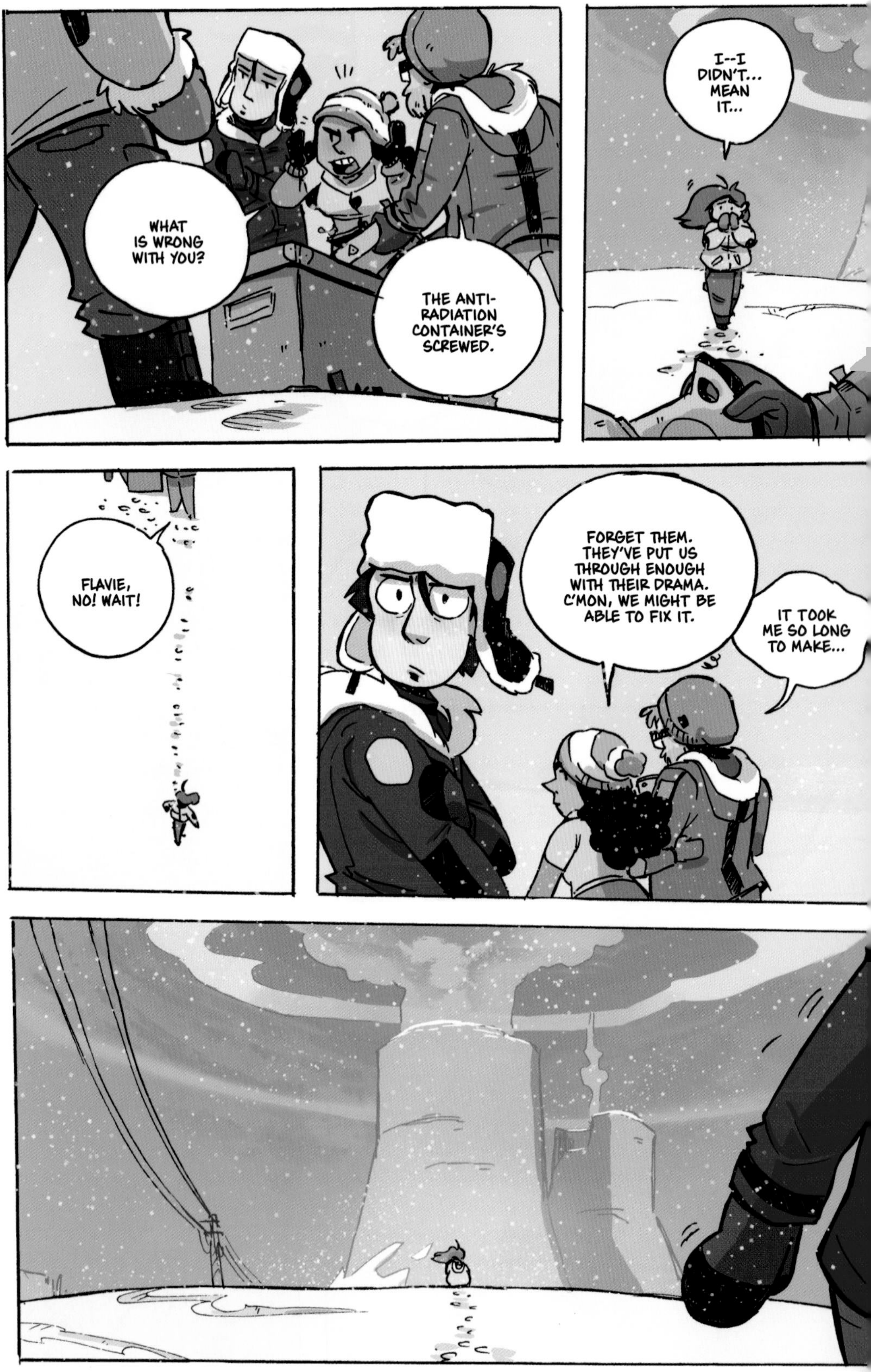
WHAT IS WRONG WITH YOU?
THE ANTI-RADIATION CONTAINER'S SCREWED.
I--I DIDN'T... MEAN IT...
FLAVIE, NO! WAIT!
FORGET THEM. THEY'VE PUT US THROUGH ENOUGH WITH THEIR DRAMA. C'MON, WE MIGHT BE ABLE TO FIX IT.
IT TOOK ME SO LONG TO MAKE...

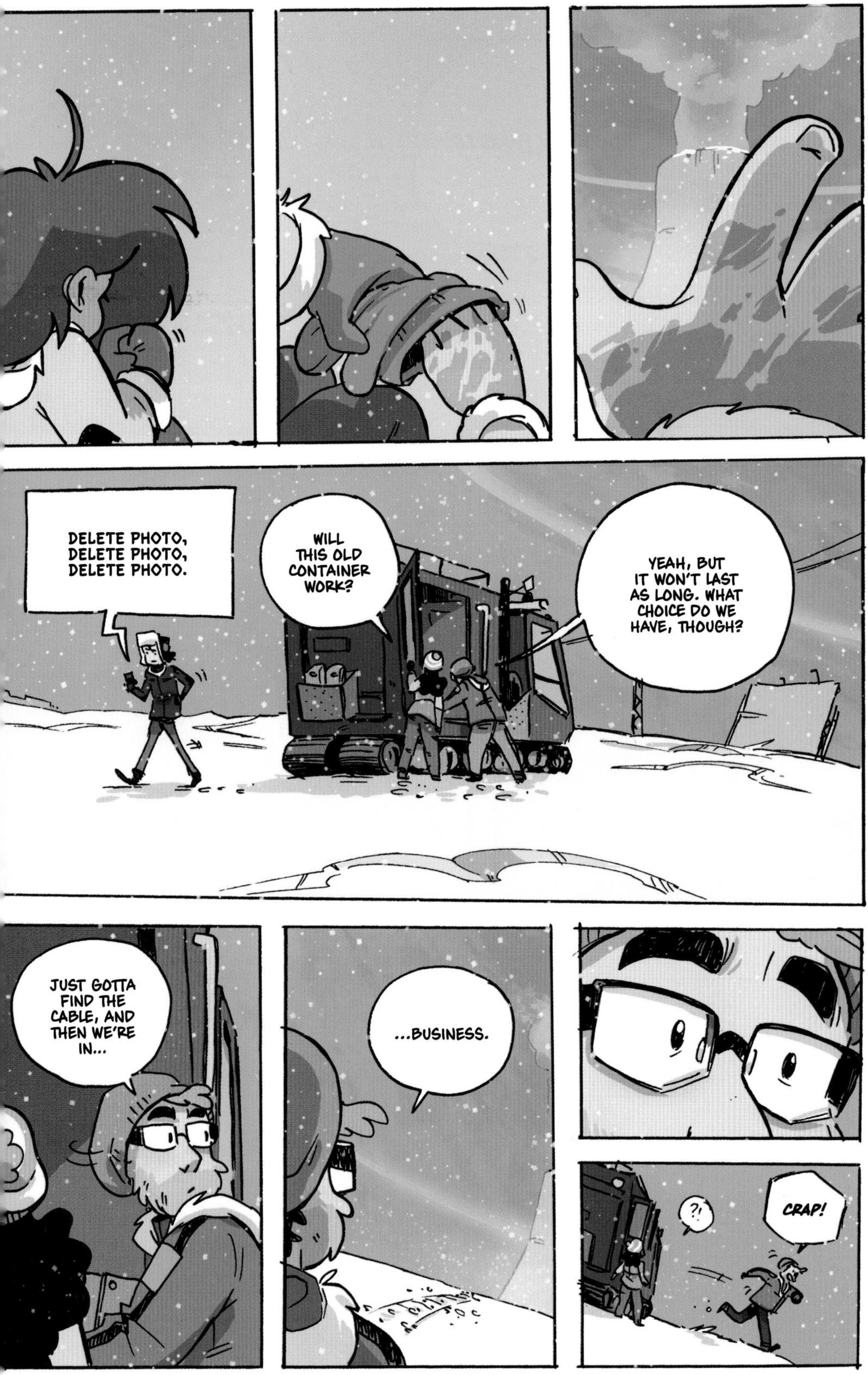
DELETE PHOTO, DELETE PHOTO, DELETE PHOTO.
WILL THIS OLD CONTAINER WORK?
YEAH, BUT IT WON'T LAST AS LONG. WHAT CHOICE DO WE HAVE, THOUGH?
JUST GOTTA FIND THE CABLE, AND THEN WE'RE IN...
...BUSINESS.
?!
CRAP!

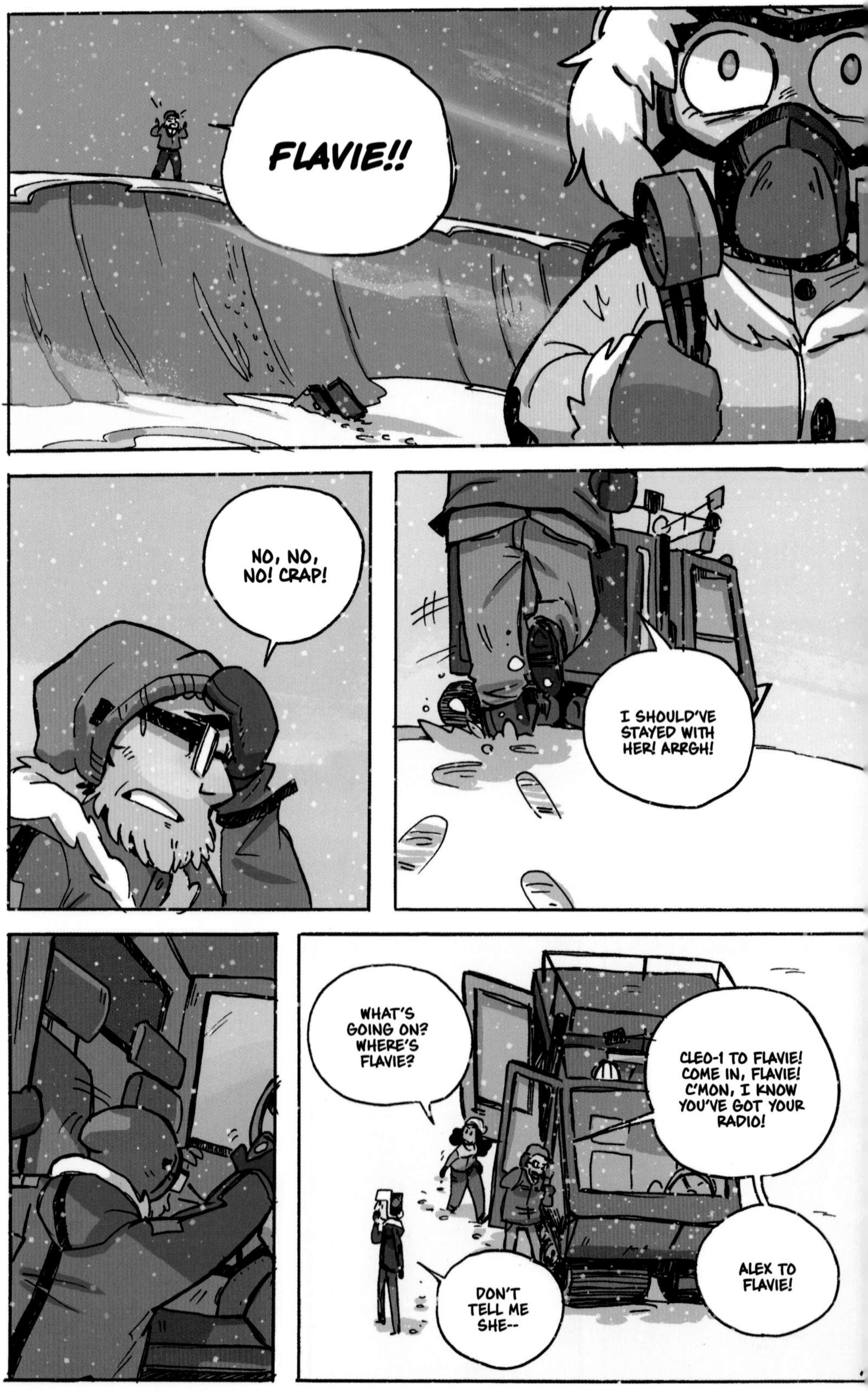
FLAVIE!!
NO, NO, NO! CRAP!
I SHOULD'VE STAYED WITH HER! ARRGH!
WHAT'S GOING ON? WHERE'S FLAVIE?
CLEO-1 TO FLAVIE! COME IN, FLAVIE! C'MON, I KNOW YOU'VE GOT YOUR RADIO!
ALEX TO FLAVIE!
DON'T TELL ME SHE--

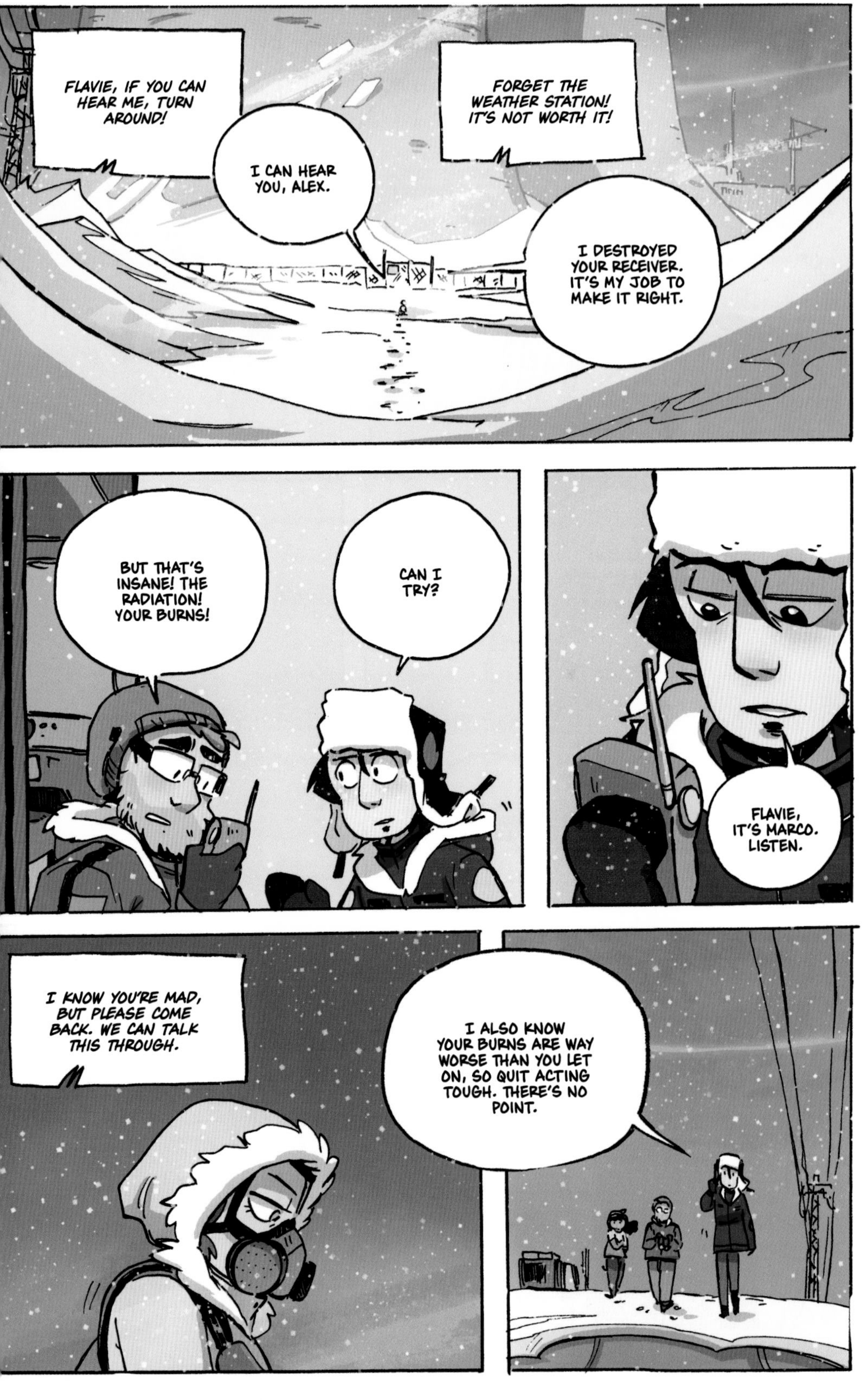
FLAVIE, IF YOU CAN HEAR ME, TURN AROUND!
I CAN HEAR YOU, ALEX.
FORGET THE WEATHER STATION! IT'S NOT WORTH IT!
I DESTROYED YOUR RECEIVER. IT'S MY JOB TO MAKE IT RIGHT.
BUT THAT'S INSANE! THE RADIATION! YOUR BURNS!
CAN I TRY?
FLAVIE, IT'S MARCO. LISTEN.
I KNOW YOU'RE MAD, BUT PLEASE COME BACK. WE CAN TALK THIS THROUGH.
I ALSO KNOW YOUR BURNS ARE WAY WORSE THAN YOU LET ON, SO QUIT ACTING TOUGH. THERE'S NO POINT.

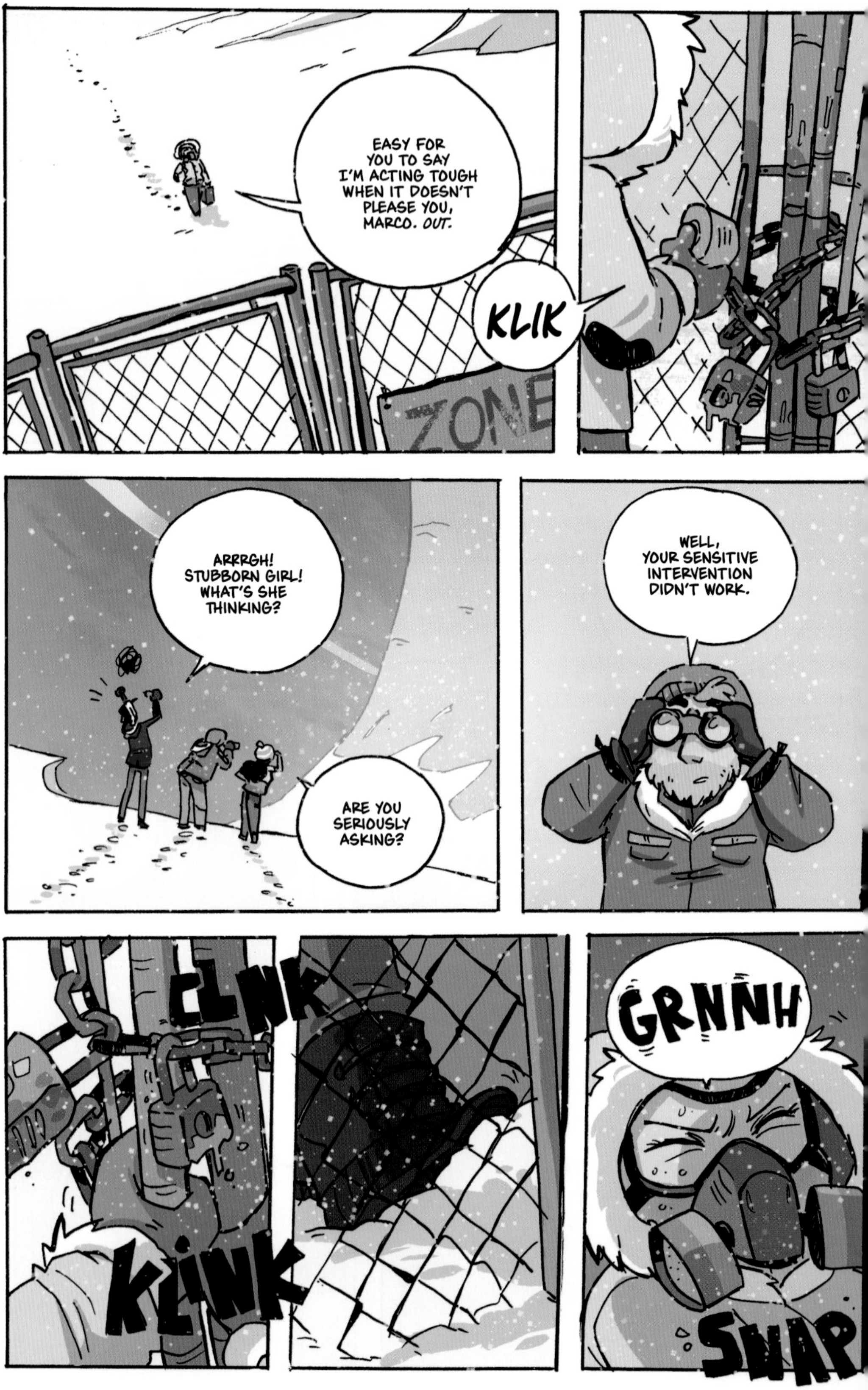

EASY FOR YOU TO SAY I'M ACTING TOUGH WHEN IT DOESN'T PLEASE YOU, MARCO. *OUT.*
KLIK
ZONE
ARRRGH! STUBBORN GIRL! WHAT'S SHE THINKING?
ARE YOU SERIOUSLY ASKING?
WELL, YOUR SENSITIVE INTERVENTION DIDN'T WORK.
CLNK
KLINK
GRNNH
SNAP

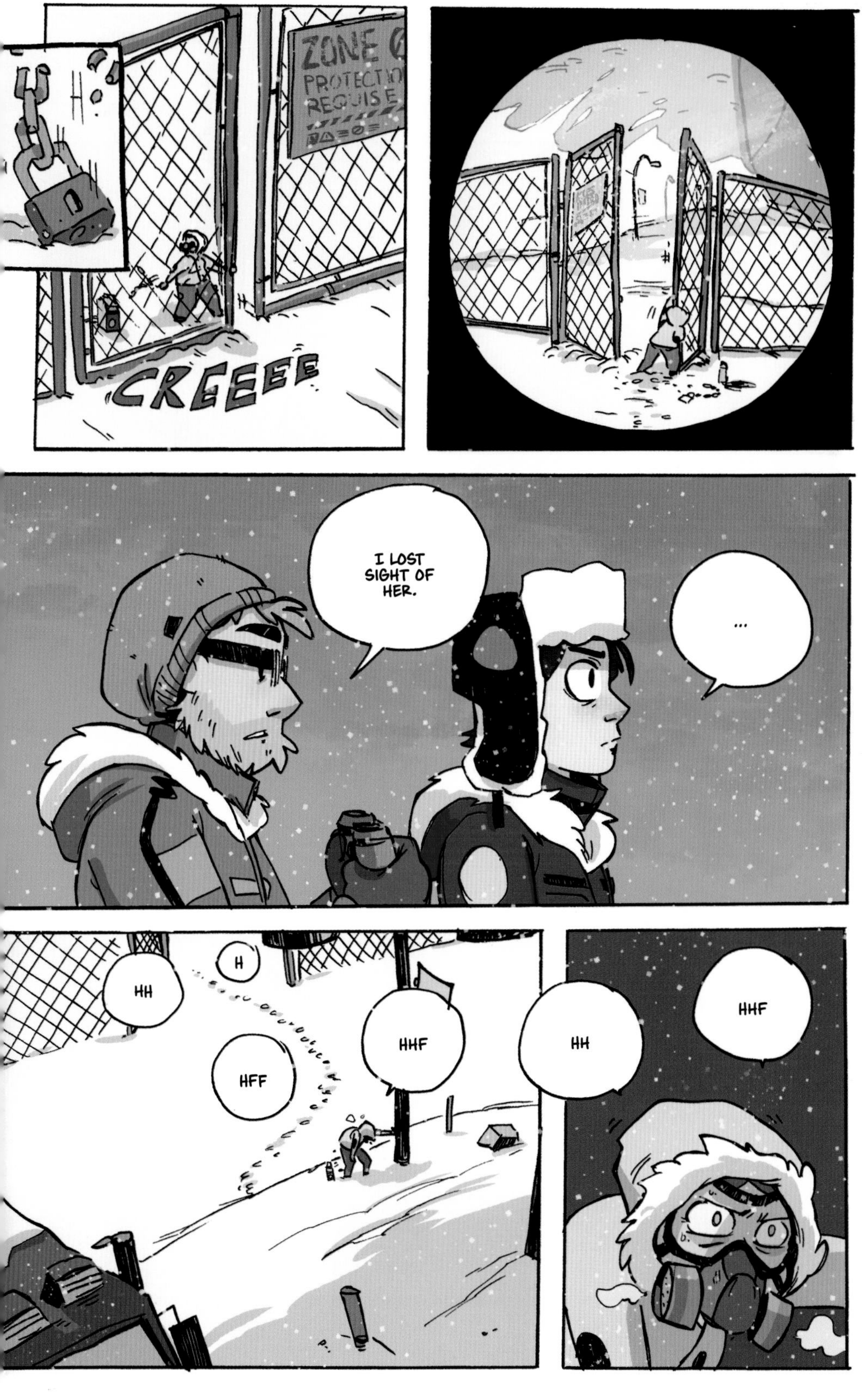
ZONE
PROTECTION
REQUISE
CREEEE
I LOST SIGHT OF HER.
...
HH
H
HFF
HHF
HH
HHF

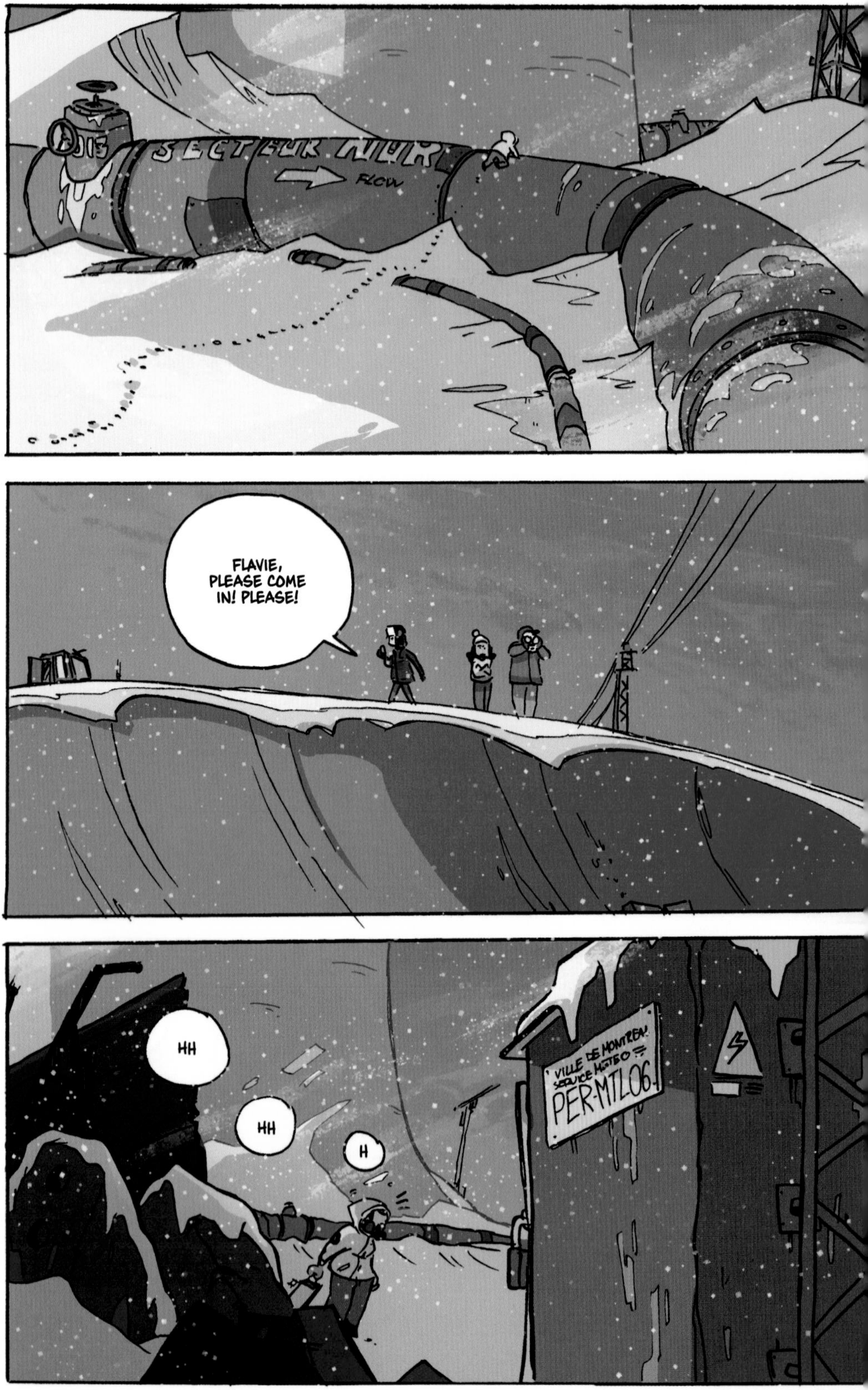
013
SECTEUR NOIR
FLOW
FLAVIE, PLEASE COME IN! PLEASE!
HH
HH
H
VILLE DE MONTREAL
PER-MTL06

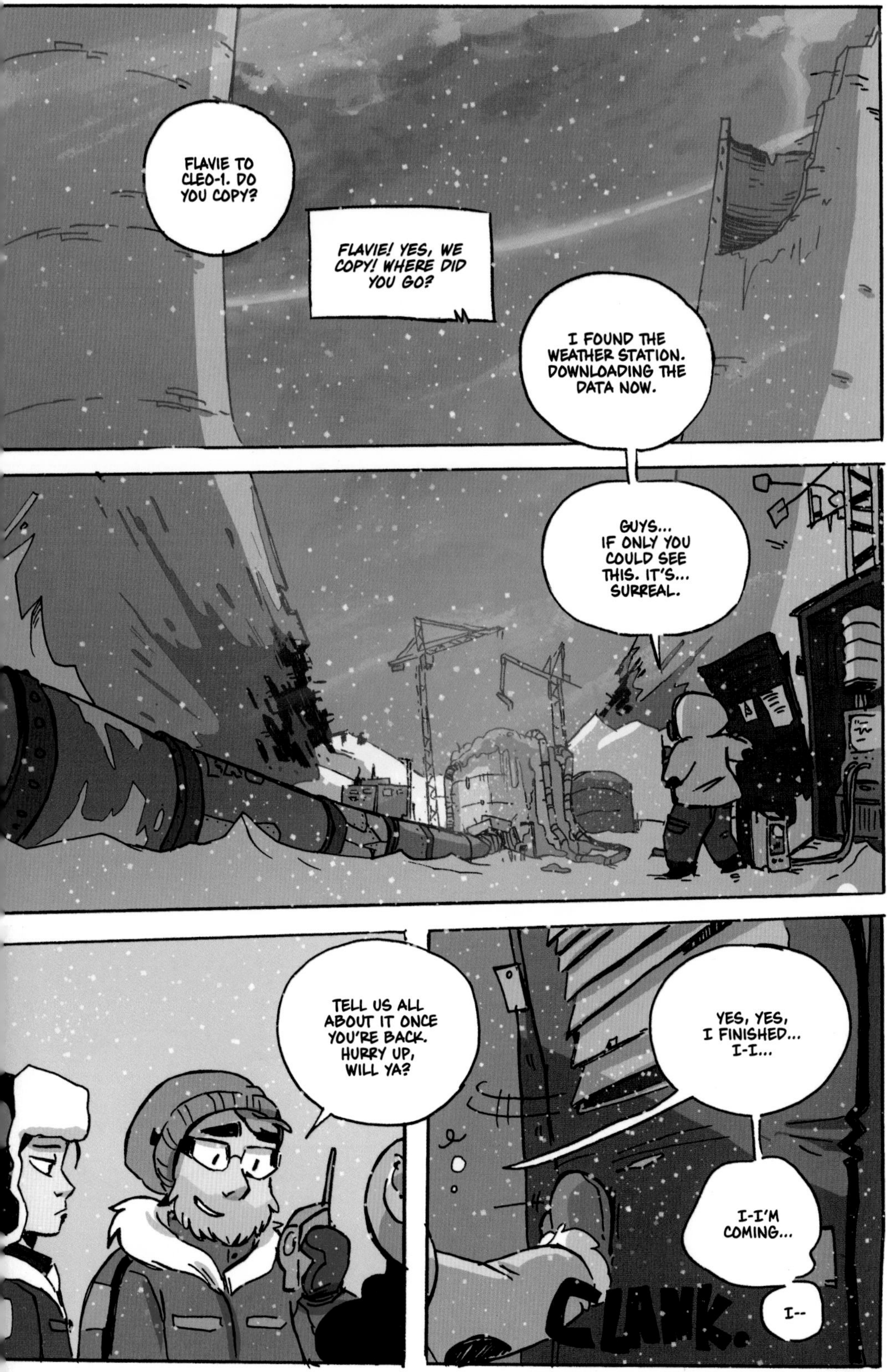
FLAVIE TO CLEO-1. DO YOU COPY?
FLAVIE! YES, WE COPY! WHERE DID YOU GO?
I FOUND THE WEATHER STATION. DOWNLOADING THE DATA NOW.
GUYS... IF ONLY YOU COULD SEE THIS. IT'S... SURREAL.
TELL US ALL ABOUT IT ONCE YOU'RE BACK. HURRY UP, WILL YA?
YES, YES, I FINISHED... I-I...
I-I'M COMING...
CLANK.
I--

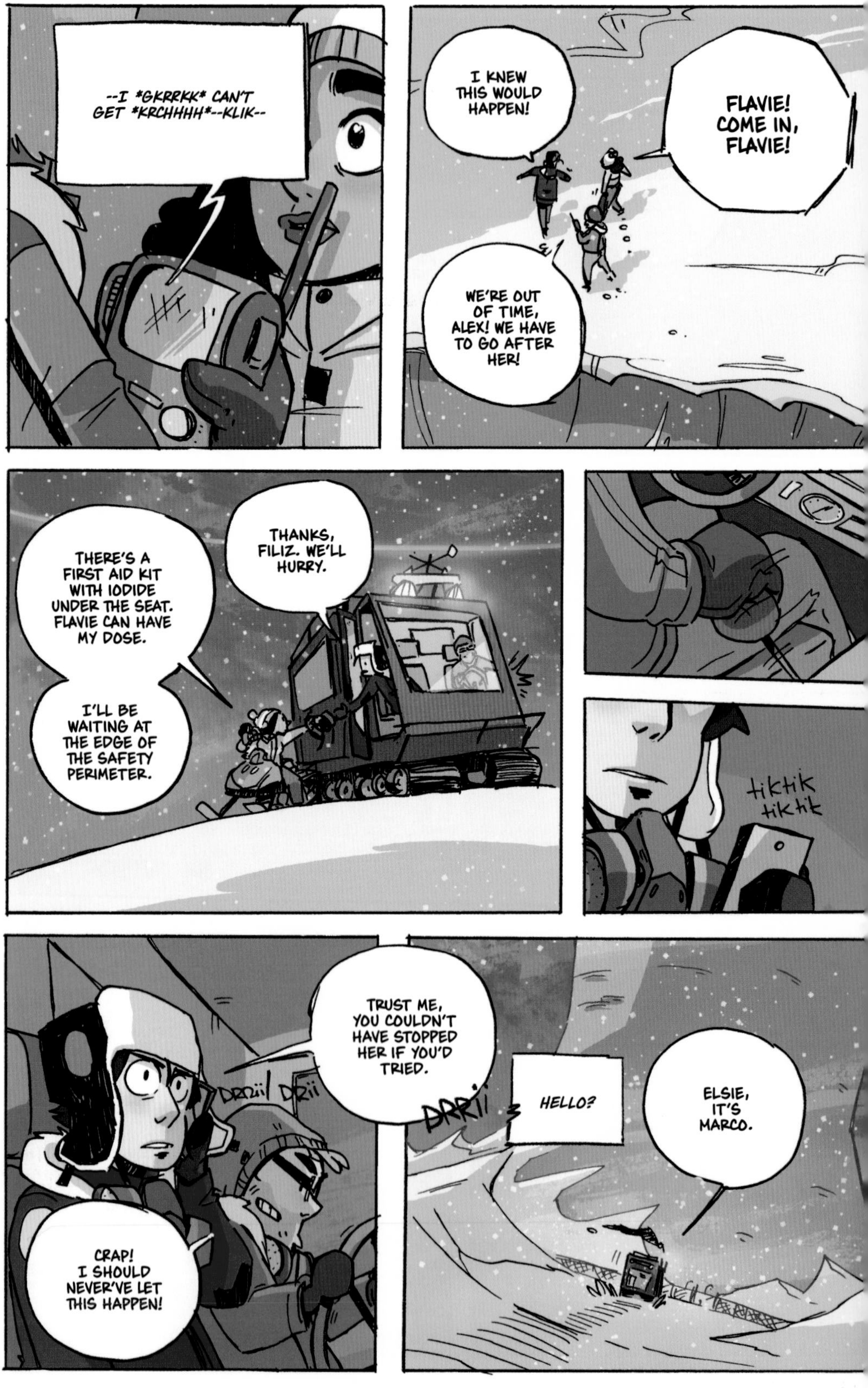
--I *GKRRKK* CAN'T GET *KRCHHHH*--KLIK--
I KNEW THIS WOULD HAPPEN!
FLAVIE! COME IN, FLAVIE!
WE'RE OUT OF TIME, ALEX! WE HAVE TO GO AFTER HER!
THERE'S A FIRST AID KIT WITH IODIDE UNDER THE SEAT. FLAVIE CAN HAVE MY DOSE.
I'LL BE WAITING AT THE EDGE OF THE SAFETY PERIMETER.
THANKS, FILIZ. WE'LL HURRY.
tiktik tiktik
DRRii DRRii
TRUST ME, YOU COULDN'T HAVE STOPPED HER IF YOU'D TRIED.
CRAP! I SHOULD NEVER'VE LET THIS HAPPEN!
DRRii
HELLO?
ELSIE, IT'S MARCO.

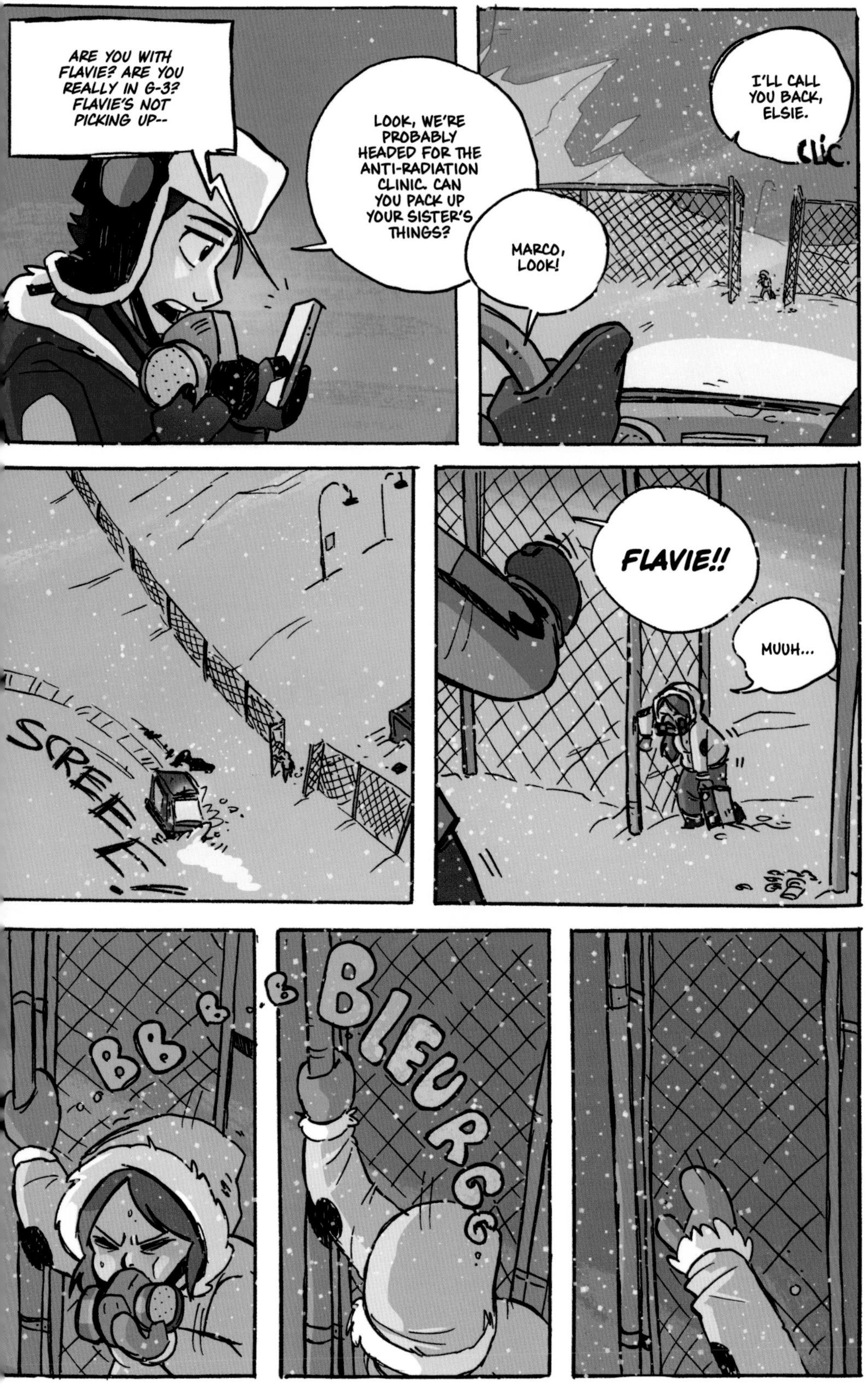
ARE YOU WITH FLAVIE? ARE YOU REALLY IN G-3? FLAVIE'S NOT PICKING UP--
LOOK, WE'RE PROBABLY HEADED FOR THE ANTI-RADIATION CLINIC. CAN YOU PACK UP YOUR SISTER'S THINGS?
MARCO, LOOK!
I'LL CALL YOU BACK, ELSIE.
CLIC.
SCREEEE!
FLAVIE!!
MUUH...
BB B B
BLEURG

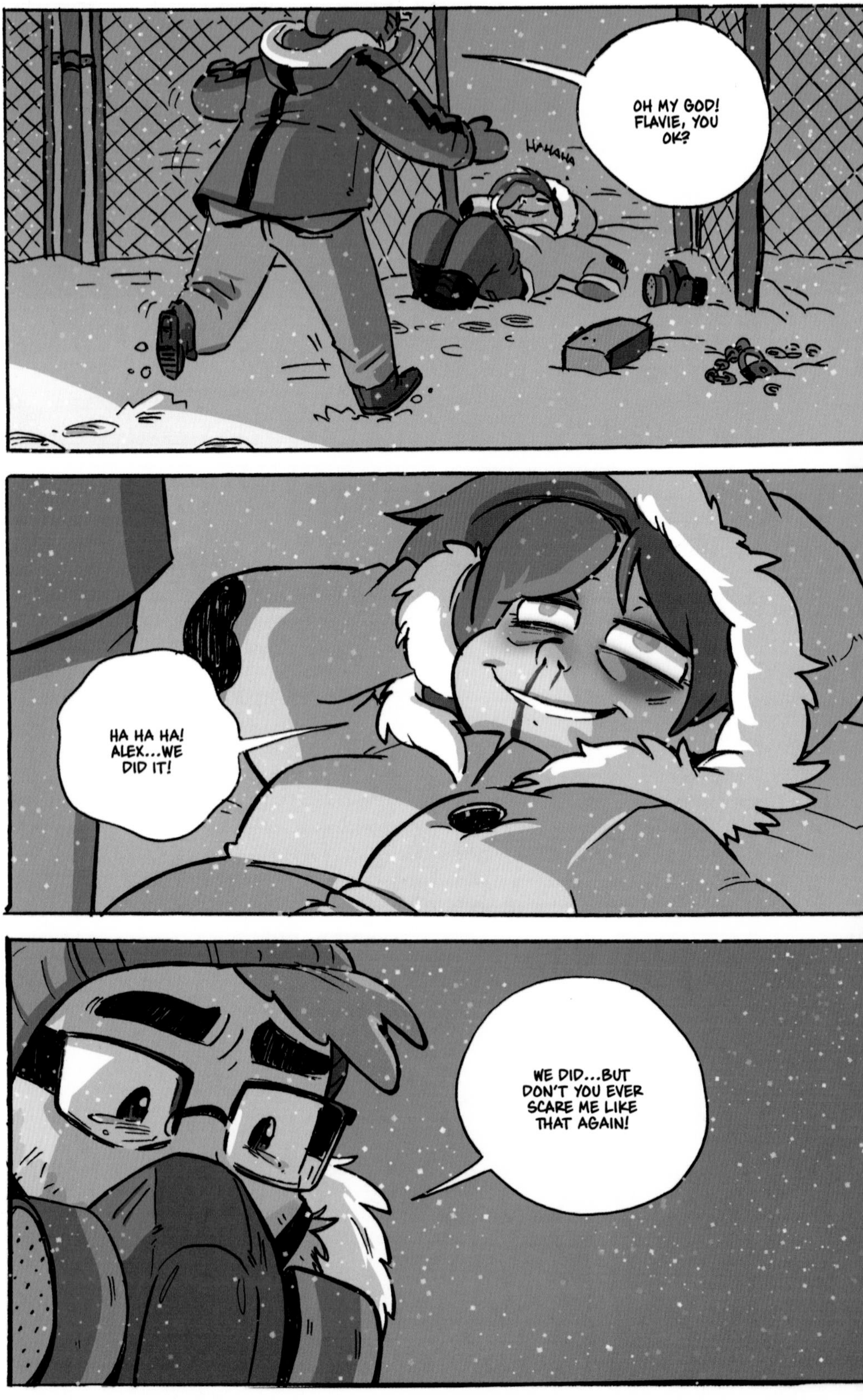
OH MY GOD! FLAVIE, YOU OK?
HAHAHA
HA HA HA! ALEX...WE DID IT!
WE DID...BUT DON'T YOU EVER SCARE ME LIKE THAT AGAIN!

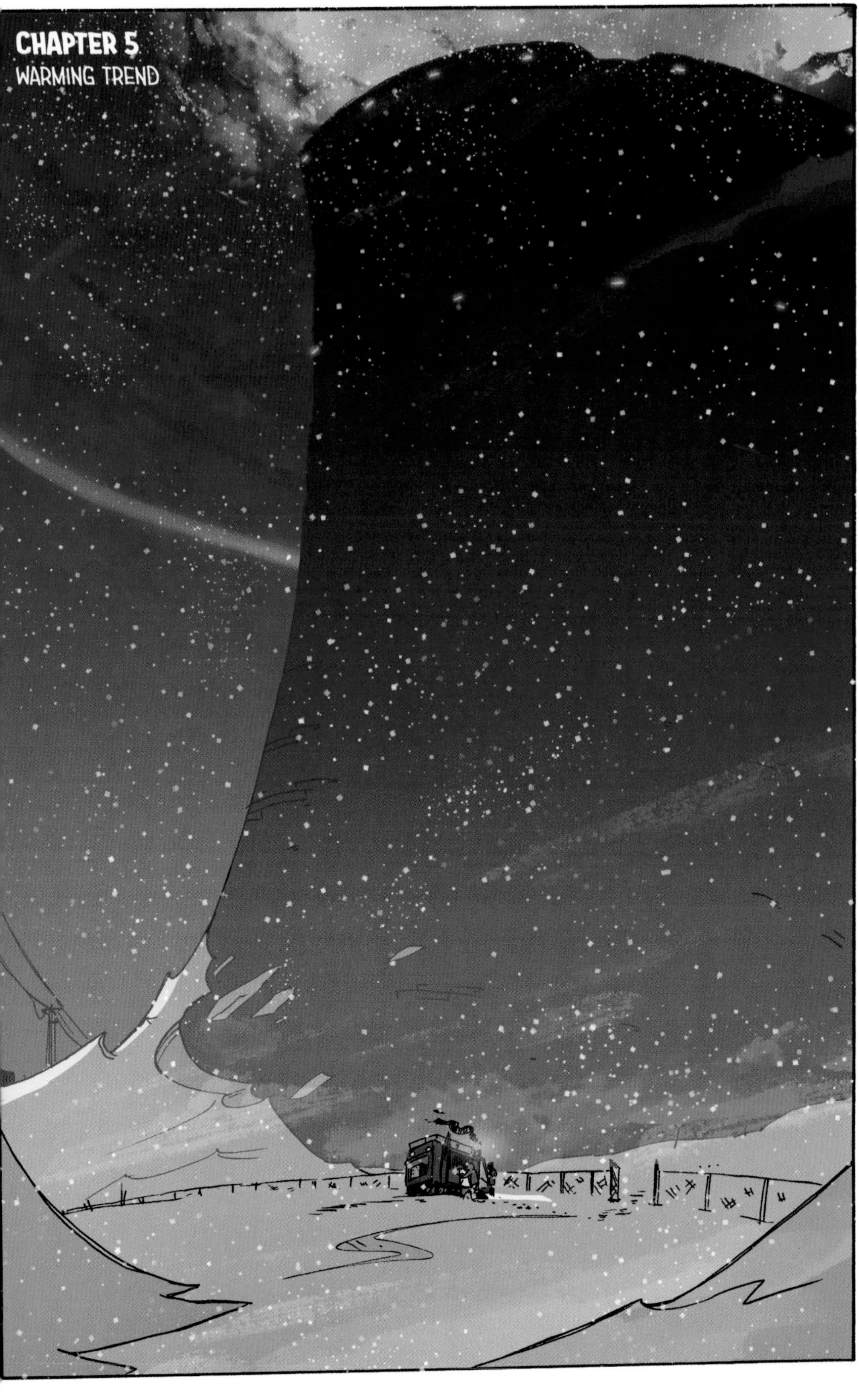
CHAPTER 5
WARMING TREND

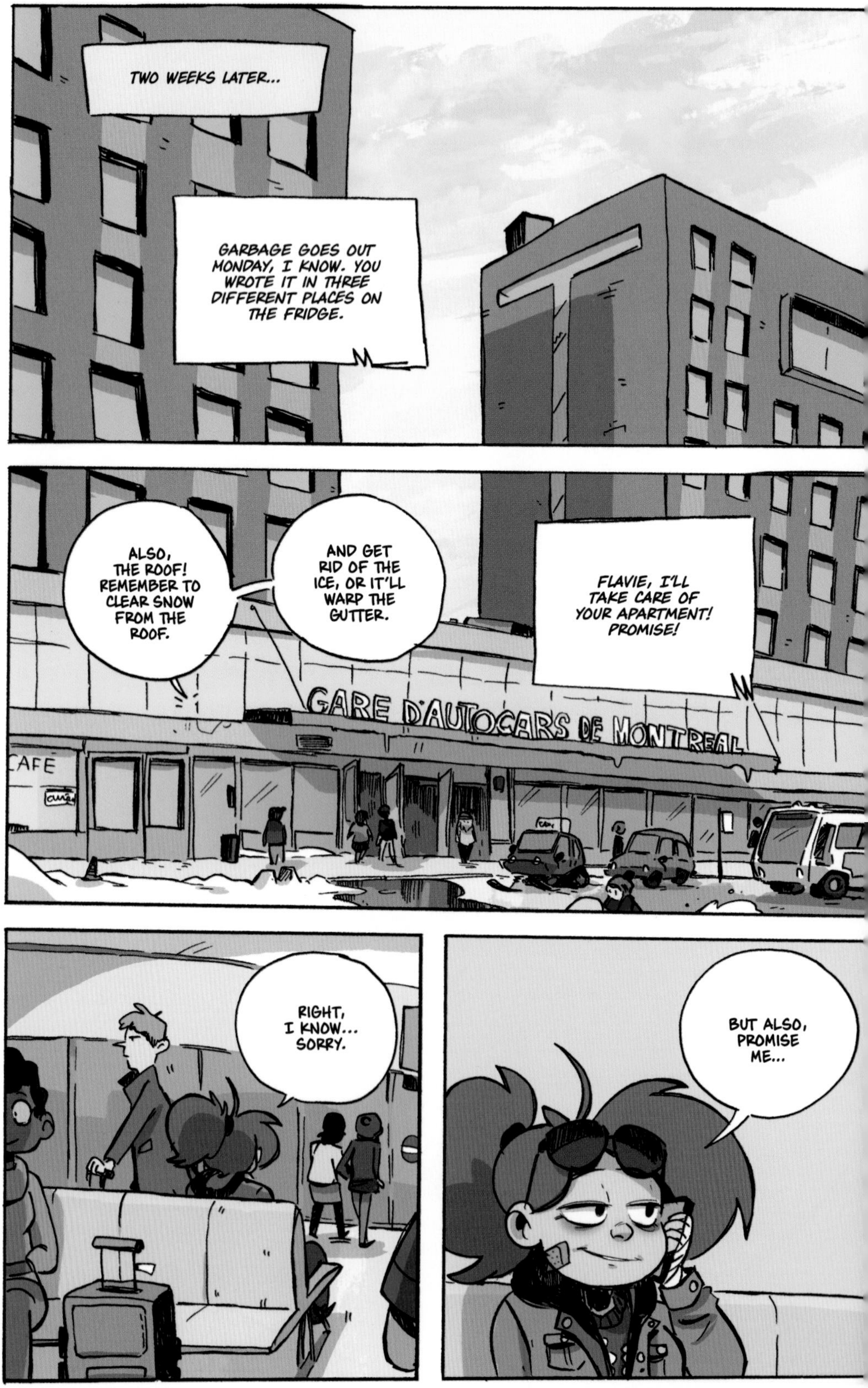
TWO WEEKS LATER...
GARBAGE GOES OUT MONDAY, I KNOW. YOU WROTE IT IN THREE DIFFERENT PLACES ON THE FRIDGE.
ALSO, THE ROOF! REMEMBER TO CLEAR SNOW FROM THE ROOF.
AND GET RID OF THE ICE, OR IT'LL WARP THE GUTTER.
FLAVIE, I'LL TAKE CARE OF YOUR APARTMENT! PROMISE!
GARE D'AUTOCARS DE MONTREAL
CAFE
RIGHT, I KNOW... SORRY.
BUT ALSO, PROMISE ME...

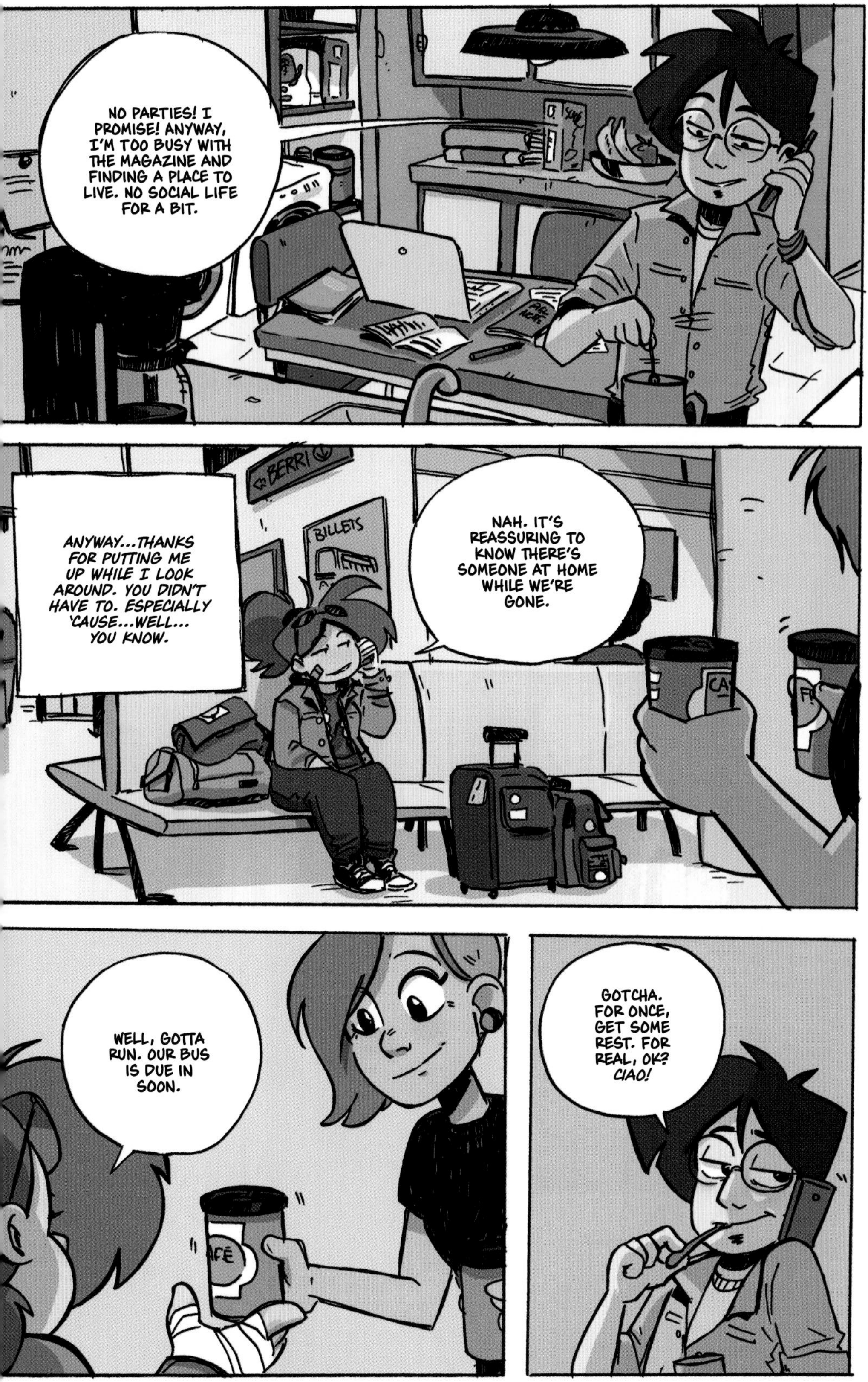
NO PARTIES! I PROMISE! ANYWAY, I'M TOO BUSY WITH THE MAGAZINE AND FINDING A PLACE TO LIVE. NO SOCIAL LIFE FOR A BIT.
BERRI
BILLETS
ANYWAY...THANKS FOR PUTTING ME UP WHILE I LOOK AROUND. YOU DIDN'T HAVE TO. ESPECIALLY 'CAUSE...WELL... YOU KNOW.
NAH. IT'S REASSURING TO KNOW THERE'S SOMEONE AT HOME WHILE WE'RE GONE.
WELL, GOTTA RUN. OUR BUS IS DUE IN SOON.
GOTCHA. FOR ONCE, GET SOME REST. FOR REAL, OK? CIAO!

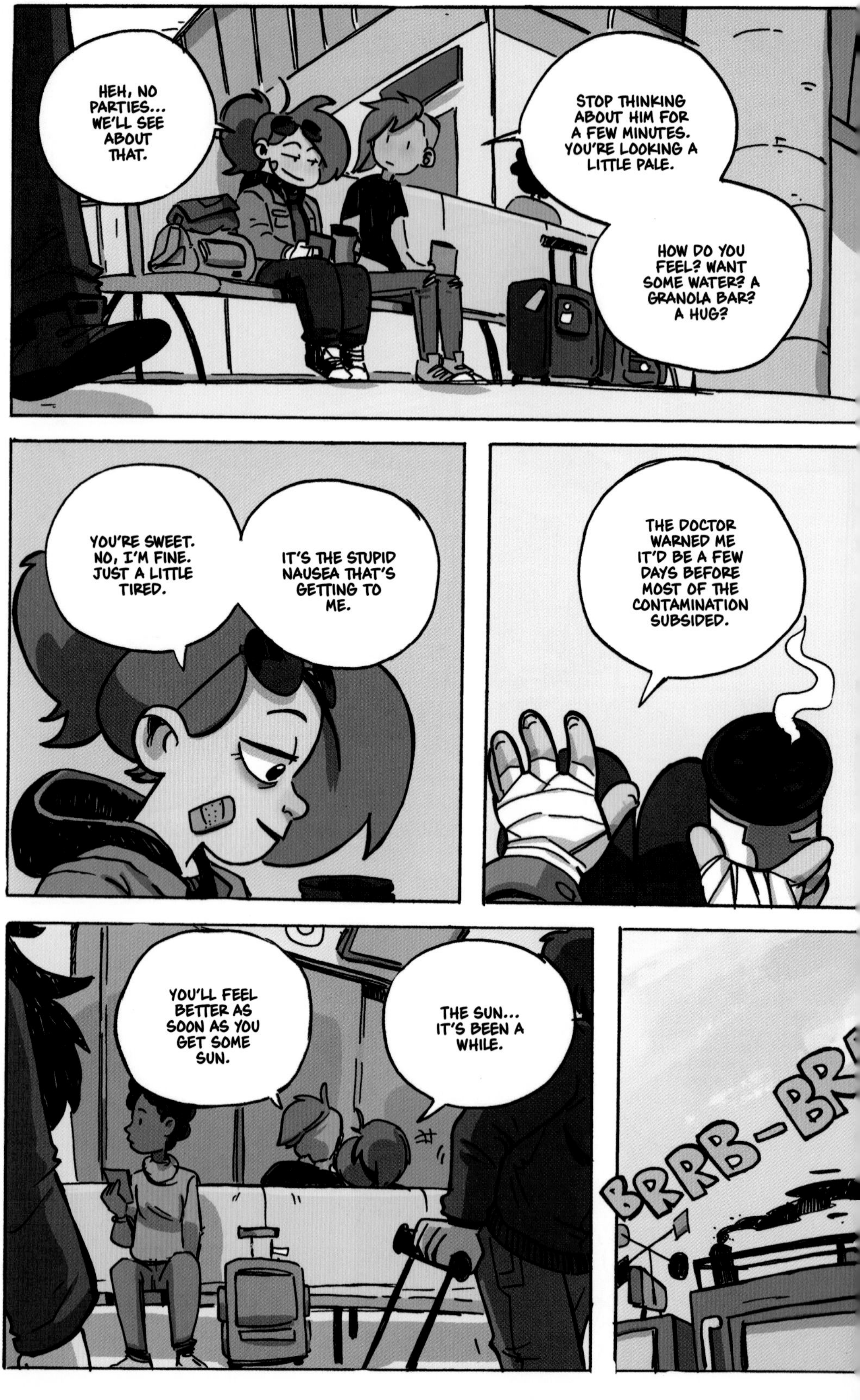
HEH, NO PARTIES... WE'LL SEE ABOUT THAT.
STOP THINKING ABOUT HIM FOR A FEW MINUTES. YOU'RE LOOKING A LITTLE PALE.
HOW DO YOU FEEL? WANT SOME WATER? A GRANOLA BAR? A HUG?
YOU'RE SWEET. NO, I'M FINE. JUST A LITTLE TIRED.
IT'S THE STUPID NAUSEA THAT'S GETTING TO ME.
THE DOCTOR WARNED ME IT'D BE A FEW DAYS BEFORE MOST OF THE CONTAMINATION SUBSIDED.
YOU'LL FEEL BETTER AS SOON AS YOU GET SOME SUN.
THE SUN... IT'S BEEN A WHILE.
BRRB-BR

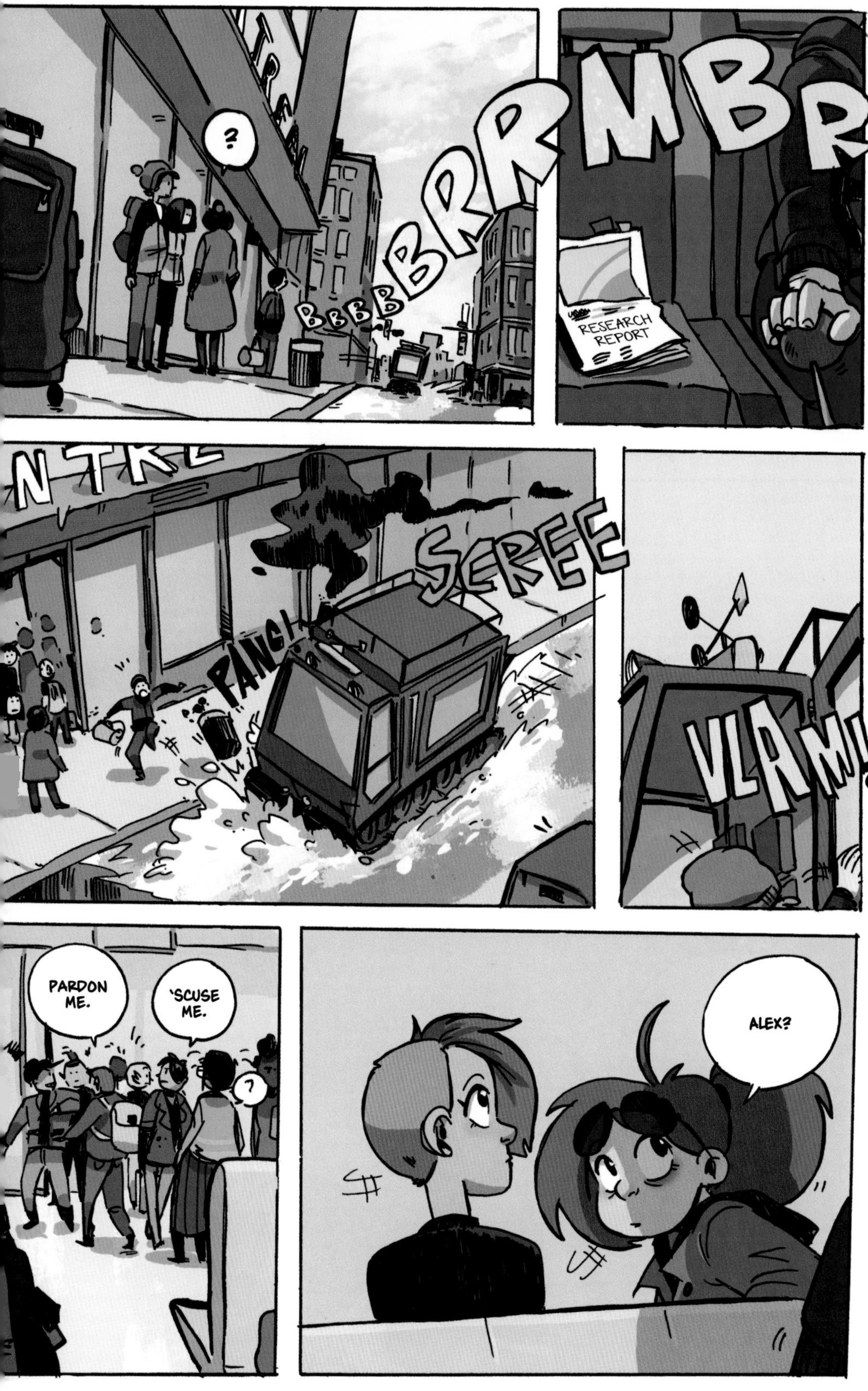
?
BBBBBRRRMBR
RESEARCH REPORT
N TRE
SCREE
PANG!
VLRAM!
PARDON ME.
'SCUSE ME.
?
ALEX?

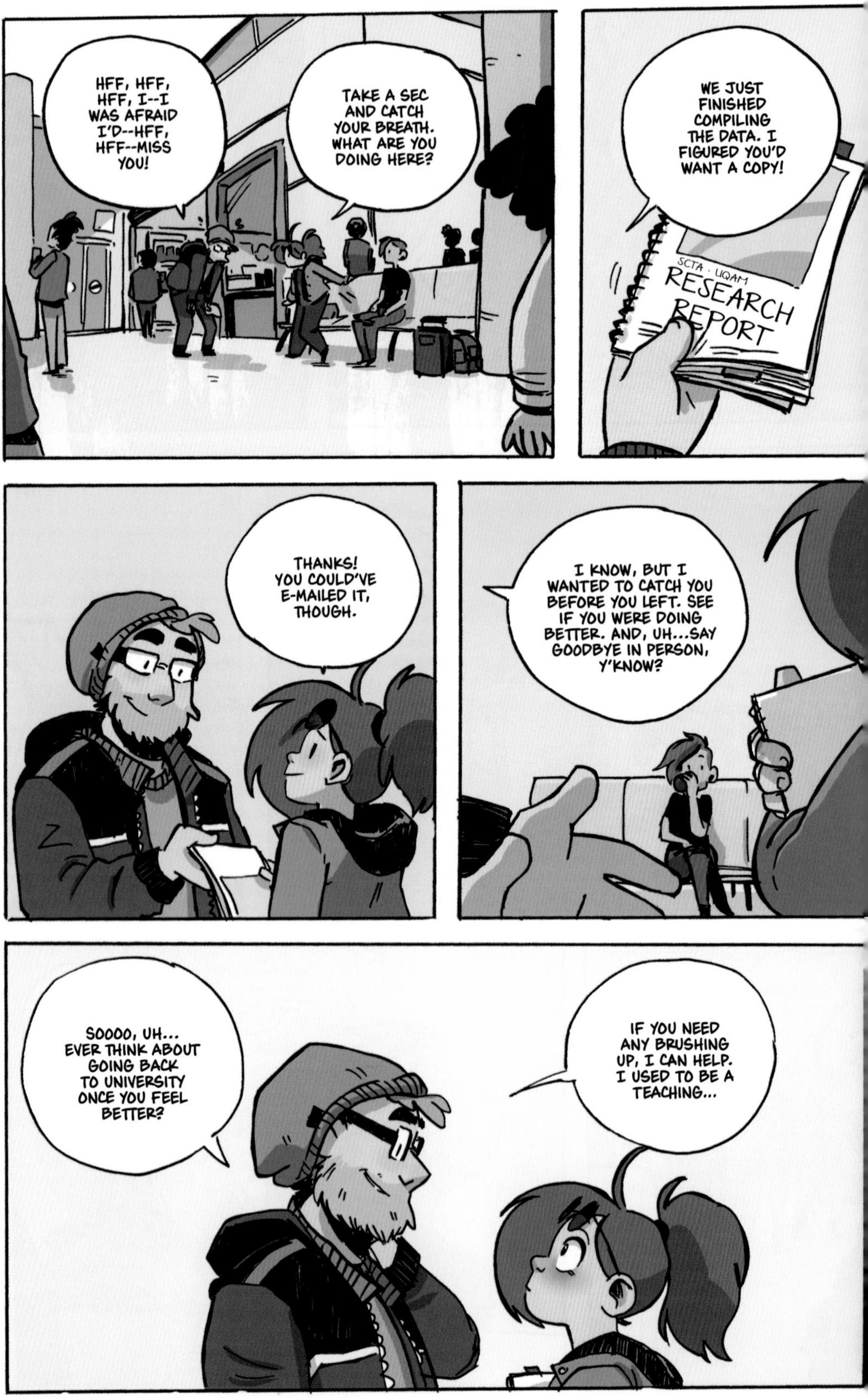
HFF, HFF, HFF, I--I WAS AFRAID I'D--HFF, HFF--MISS YOU!
TAKE A SEC AND CATCH YOUR BREATH. WHAT ARE YOU DOING HERE?
WE JUST FINISHED COMPILING THE DATA. I FIGURED YOU'D WANT A COPY!
SCTA · UQAM
RESEARCH REPORT
THANKS! YOU COULD'VE E-MAILED IT, THOUGH.
I KNOW, BUT I WANTED TO CATCH YOU BEFORE YOU LEFT. SEE IF YOU WERE DOING BETTER. AND, UH...SAY GOODBYE IN PERSON, Y'KNOW?
SOOOO, UH... EVER THINK ABOUT GOING BACK TO UNIVERSITY ONCE YOU FEEL BETTER?
IF YOU NEED ANY BRUSHING UP, I CAN HELP. I USED TO BE A TEACHING...

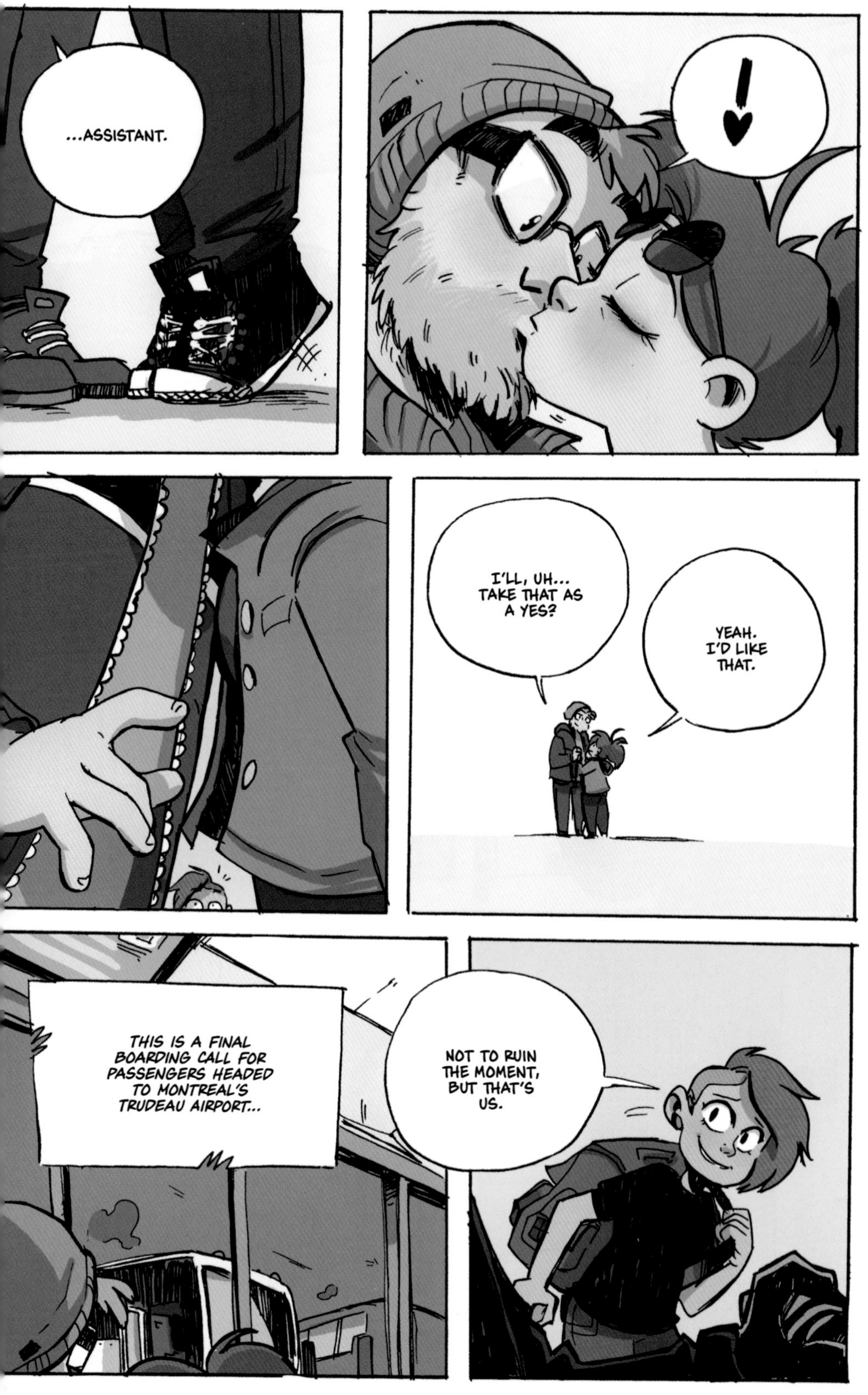
...ASSISTANT.
!♥
I'LL, UH... TAKE THAT AS A YES?
YEAH. I'D LIKE THAT.
THIS IS A FINAL BOARDING CALL FOR PASSENGERS HEADED TO MONTREAL'S TRUDEAU AIRPORT...
NOT TO RUIN THE MOMENT, BUT THAT'S US.

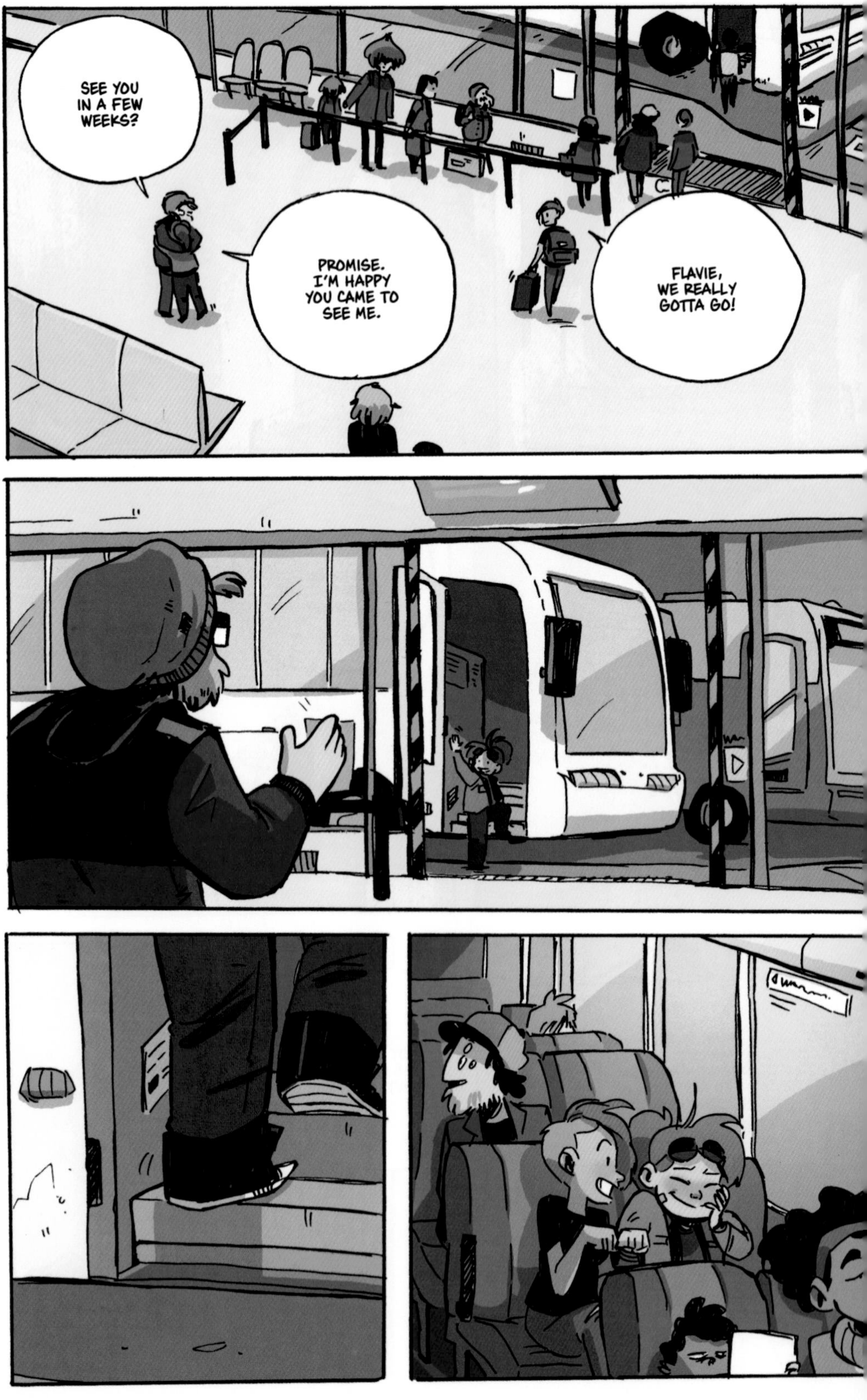
SEE YOU IN A FEW WEEKS?
PROMISE. I'M HAPPY YOU CAME TO SEE ME.
FLAVIE, WE REALLY GOTTA GO!

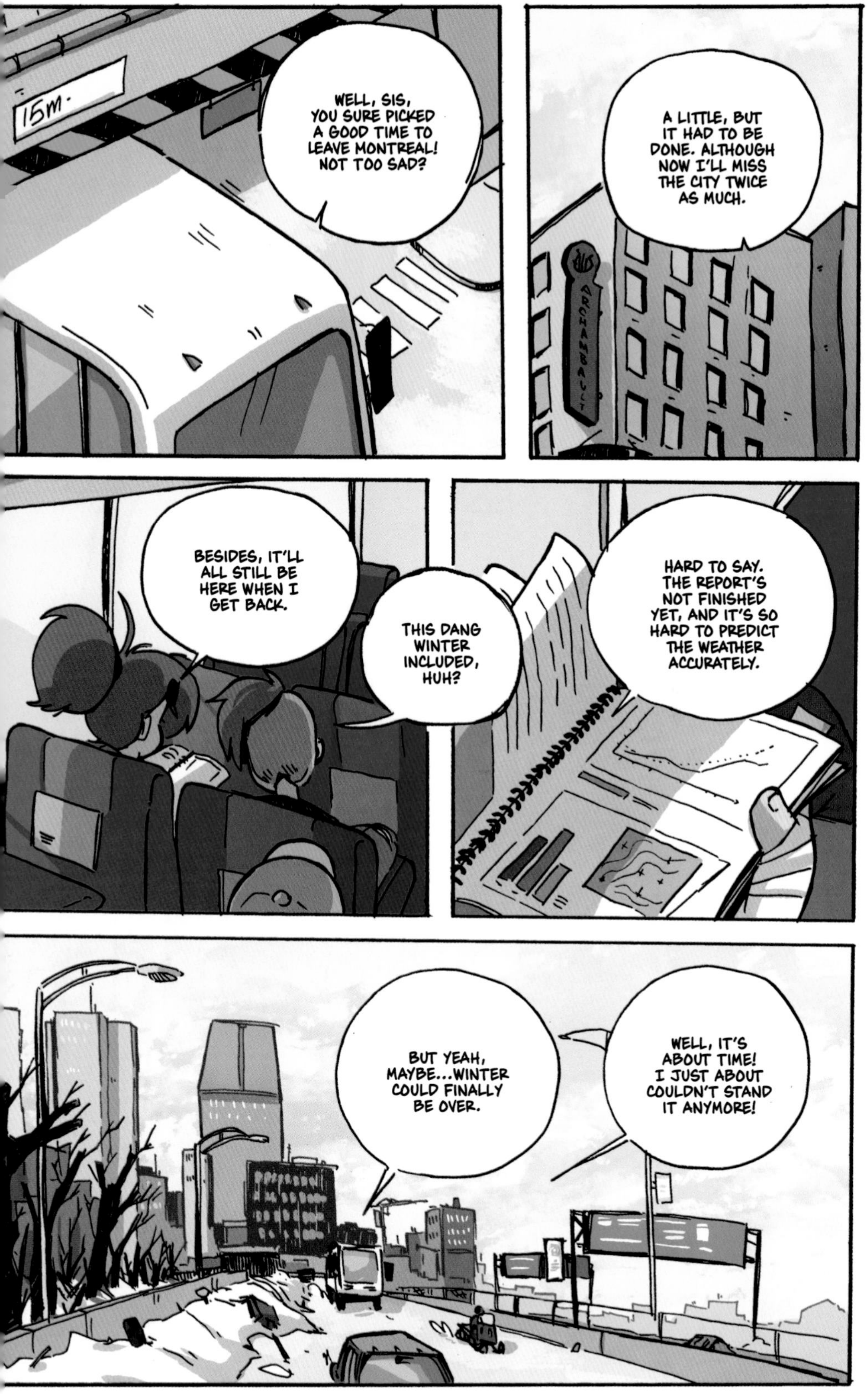
15m.
WELL, SIS, YOU SURE PICKED A GOOD TIME TO LEAVE MONTREAL! NOT TOO SAD?
A LITTLE, BUT IT HAD TO BE DONE. ALTHOUGH NOW I'LL MISS THE CITY TWICE AS MUCH.
ARCHAMBAULT
BESIDES, IT'LL ALL STILL BE HERE WHEN I GET BACK.
THIS DANG WINTER INCLUDED, HUH?
HARD TO SAY. THE REPORT'S NOT FINISHED YET, AND IT'S SO HARD TO PREDICT THE WEATHER ACCURATELY.
BUT YEAH, MAYBE...WINTER COULD FINALLY BE OVER.
WELL, IT'S ABOUT TIME! I JUST ABOUT COULDN'T STAND IT ANYMORE!

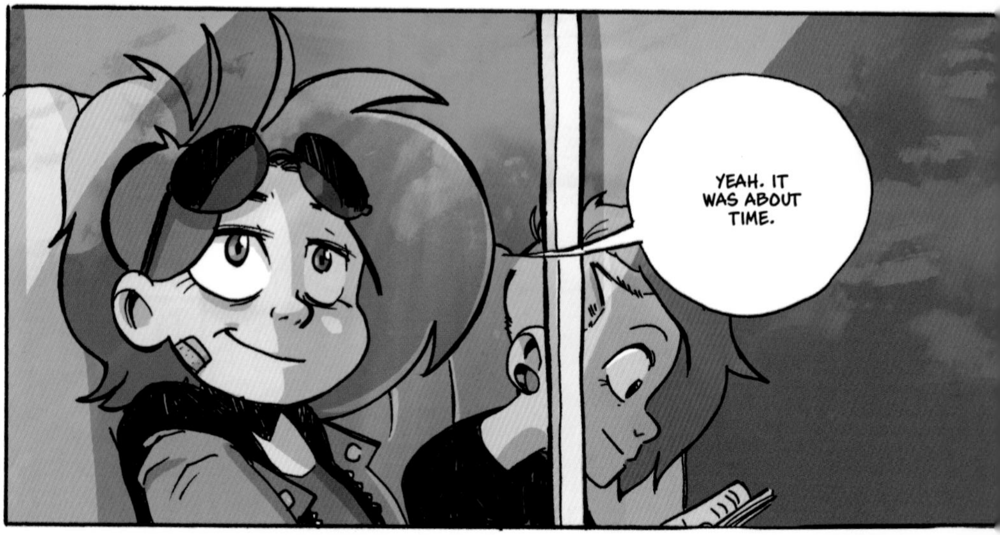
YEAH. IT WAS ABOUT TIME.

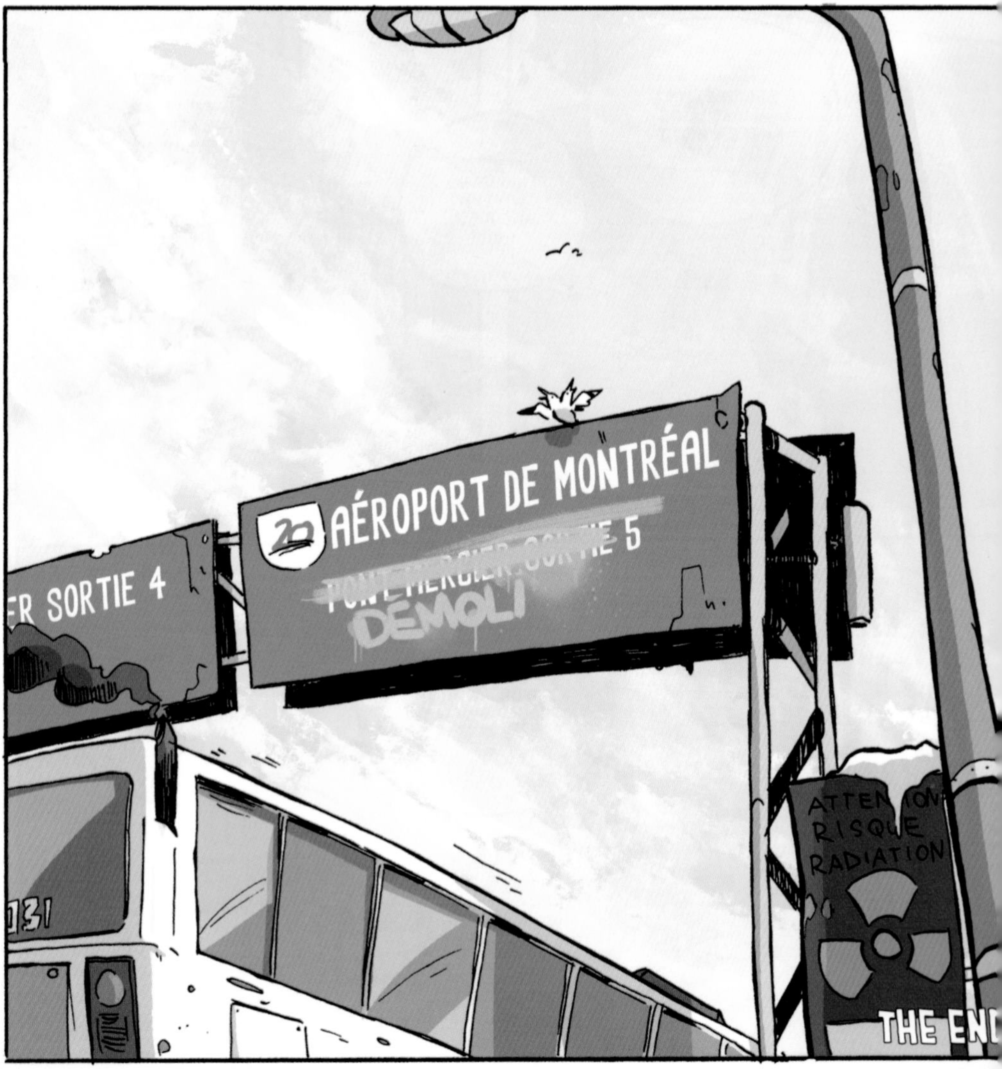
ER SORTIE 4
20 AÉROPORT DE MONTRÉAL
PONT MERCIER SORTIE 5
DEMOLI
ATTEN ION
RISQUE
RADIATION
031
THE EN

ABOUT THE AUTHOR

Caroline Breault (aka Cab) is a comic artist based in Montreal and the creator of the graphic novel series Hiver Nucléaire (aka "Nuclear Winter"). A full-time resident at Lounak Studios, she also works as a colorist and a freelance illustrator. In 2017, Cab received a nomination for the Joe Shuster Awards for best cartoonist. In reality, she does not like winter one bit but thinks it looks really pretty.

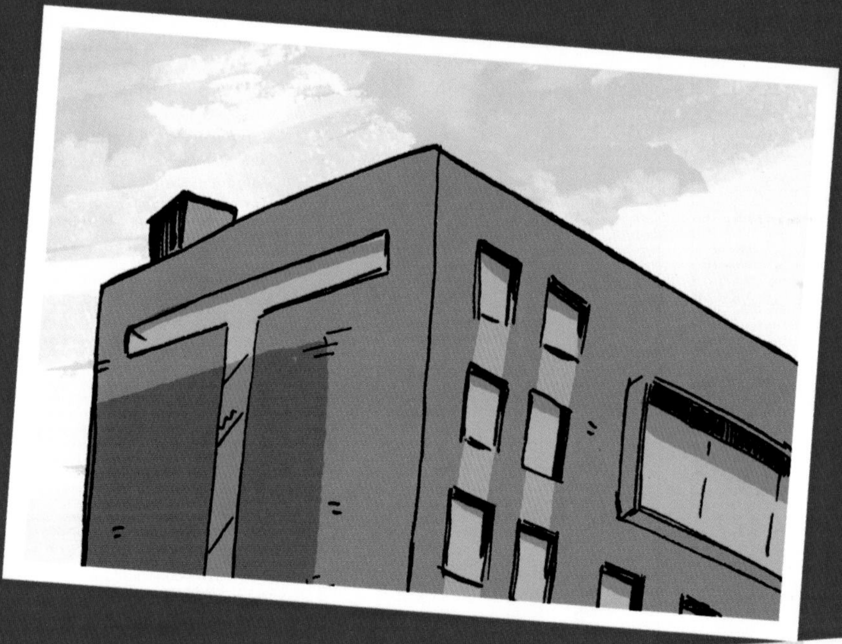

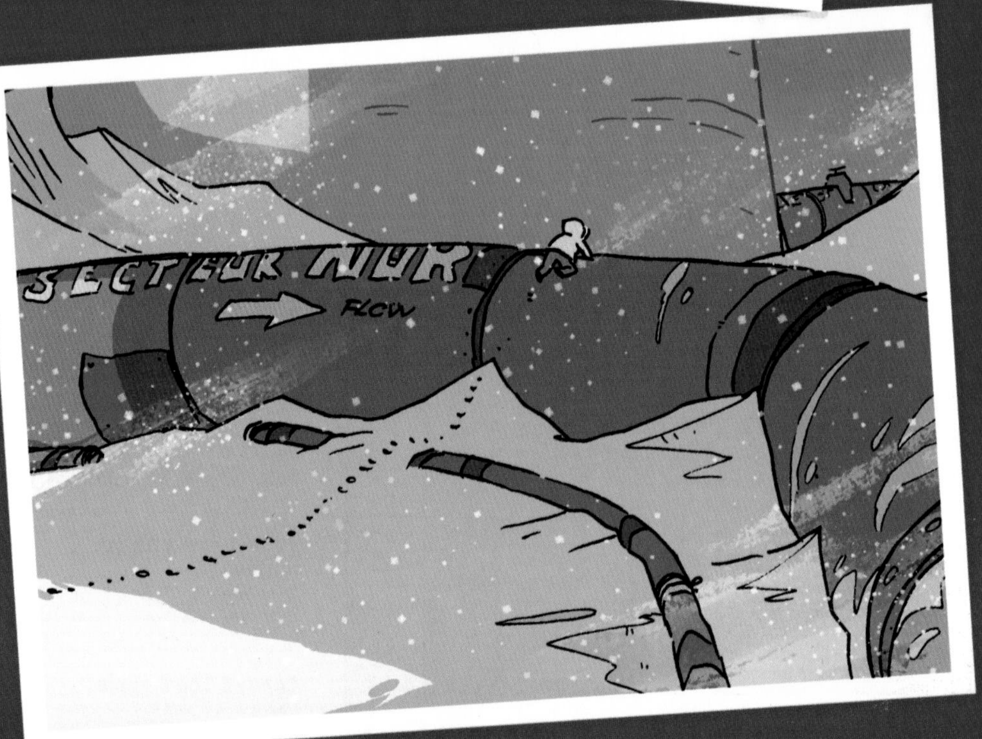
SECTEUR
FLOW

DISCOVER
ALL THE HITS

STEVENSON • ELLIS • WATTERS • ALLEN
LUMBERJANES
BEWARE THE KITTEN HOLY
NEW YORK TIMES BESTSELLING SERIES

Allison + Treiman + Cogar
GIANT DAYS
VOLUME ONE

RIBON • FISH • PEER
SLAM!
VOLUME ONE

Hope Larson • Brittney Williams • Sarah Stern
GOLDIE VANCE
Volume One

THE BACKSTAGERS

TYSON HESSE'S
DIESEL
IGNITION

BOOM! BOX

AVAILABLE AT YOUR LOCAL COMICS SHOP AND BOOKSTORE

To find a comics shop in your area, call 1-888-266-4226

WWW.**BOOM-STUDIOS**.COM

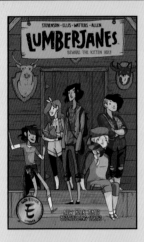

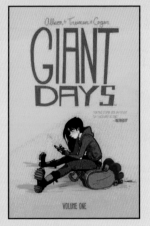

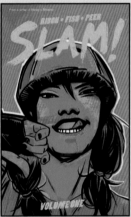

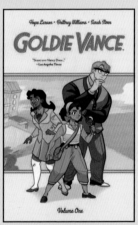

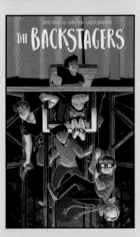

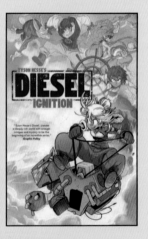

Lumberjanes
Noelle Stevenson, Shannon Watters, Grace Ellis, Brooklyn Allen, and Others
Volume 1: Beware the Kitten Holy
ISBN: 978-1-60886-687-8 | $14.99 US
Volume 2: Friendship to the Max
ISBN: 978-1-60886-737-0 | $14.99 US
Volume 3: A Terrible Plan
ISBN: 978-1-60886-803-2 | $14.99 US
Volume 4: Out of Time
ISBN: 978-1-60886-860-5 | $14.99 US
Volume 5: Band Together
ISBN: 978-1-60886-919-0 | $14.99 US

Giant Days
John Allison, Lissa Treiman, Max Sarin
Volume 1
ISBN: 978-1-60886-789-9 | $9.99 US
Volume 2
ISBN: 978-1-60886-804-9 | $14.99 US
Volume 3
ISBN: 978-1-60886-851-3 | $14.99 US

Jonesy
Sam Humphries, Caitlin Rose Boyle
Volume 1
ISBN: 978-1-60886-883-4 | $9.99 US
Volume 2
ISBN: 978-1-60886-999-2 | $14.99 US

Slam!
Pamela Ribon, Veronica Fish, Brittany Peer
Volume 1
ISBN: 978-1-68415-004-5 | $14.99 US

Goldie Vance
Hope Larson, Brittney Williams
Volume 1
ISBN: 978-1-60886-898-8 | $9.99 US
Volume 2
ISBN: 978-1-60886-974-9 | $14.99 US

The Backstagers
James Tynion IV, Rian Sygh
Volume 1
ISBN: 978-1-60886-993-0 | $14.99 US

Tyson Hesse's Diesel: Ignition
Tyson Hesse
ISBN: 978-1-60886-907-7 | $14.99 US

Coady & The Creepies
Liz Prince, Amanda Kirk, Hannah Fisher
ISBN: 978-1-68415-029-8 | $14.99 US